The H.O.P.E. Story

The HOPE Story

A Story and Study of Supportive Groups and Their Guides

Kenneth Hawley Hamilton MD, CM

Joyce Oetinger Murphy RN, MSN, AHN-BC

©2007 HOPE Healing Publications
PO Box 276, 52 High St.
South Paris, ME 04281-0276
(207) 743-7458
http://www.hope@hopehealing.org

ISBN 0-9725760-2-9 $19.95

Hope is the thing with feathers
That perches in the soul,
And sings the tune without the words,
And never stops at all,

And sweetest in the gale is heard;
And sore must be the storm
That could abash the little bird
That kept so many warm.

I've heard it in the chillest land,
And on the strangest sea;
Yet, never, in extremity,
It asked a crumb of me.

  Emily Dickinson; XXXIII.

Hope is in place precisely in the face of evil that tempts us to despair, and more especially that evil that belongs specifically to our own age and condition. The presupposition of hope is, therefore, belief in a reality that transcends what is available as evidence.

  Alistair MacIntyre, Seven Traits for Designing Our Descendants, Hastings Center Report 9 (1979): 5-7.

Acknowledgements

This work is possible only because of the willing cooperation of so many HOPE Group participants who were generously comfortable with Joyce's presence and meticulous note-taking. In her presence, these fine "persons exceptional" felt comfortable and safe. We are especially grateful to those who have shared their personal stories with Joyce. Ken was not present in any of those interviews, and because of his familiarity and friendship with those who were interviewed, he was able to identify each donor. Both of us feel deeply grateful for all that we have been given.

HOPE's Board of Directors, HOPErs all, have been generous with their support for this project. HOPE's Action Committee, comprised of Charleen Chase, Denver Whisman, Gail Brusoe, Jean Libbey, Joanna Leary, Kathy Brummer, Sue Vangeli, Theresa Quinn, and Robert Cromwell, have all contributed wonderful thoughts. We also thank our professional reviewers: Fred Craigie, Ph.D.; Laura Thompson-Brady, Ph.D. candidate; and Kevin Wallace, M.D., for their clear observations and valuable contributions.

The lovely cover background is a photo, "Ducks at Dawn, North Pond," by Murad Saÿen and used with his permission and blessing. The HOPE logo is the design work of his son, Sam Saÿen.

Table of Contents

Preface

This is the story of H.O.P.E., Healing of Persons Exceptional (HOPE). Common dictionary definitions of the word, "hope," express the concept of a positive desired outcome. This book is the story of another form of hope—that which affirms life as inherently meaningful. This form is the foundation of supportive HOPE Groups and their twenty-year history. The story of HOPE is a synthesis of the people whose lives have been touched by its gifts and who, in turn, have shared their gifts within the safety of this community. In the words of Kenneth H. Hamilton M. D. (2005), HOPE's founder:

> "HOPE Groups are gatherings of people who come together to find wellness by replacing fear with hope—the key to deepening the meaning, value and purpose of their lives.... They are catalysts of change where the attitude is HOPE—the attitude of meaning and possibility—and their context is love, that of true relationships.(p. 1)"

HOPE's story is a dedication to these people, living and passed, and to those among them who devoted themselves to others through the role of the HOPE Guide. HOPE's story is dedicated to Dr. Hamilton and the people who have served on the Board of Directors of H.O.P.E., Incorporated, over the last twenty years.

This book's purpose is to bring to light the individual and shared experiences of people who have participated in HOPE. It proposes to invite you, the reader, to witness the stories of those who have come to call themselves HOPErs. Read their words, breathe in their wisdom, and reflect upon how the presence of HOPE might contribute to your life or that of someone whom you love or serve.

And, to empower the reader's thinking about hope and HOPE, we encourage you to look at hope through the soul of Vaclav Havel, Czech playwright and poet, "(hope) is not the conviction that something will turn out well, but the certainty that

something makes sense, regardless of how it turns out"
(Symynkywicz). It is this form of hope that kept survivors alive
through the deep suffering of Hitler's concentration camps (Frankl,
1992). It is this form of hope that carries people through the
suffering of our most serious and life-threatening physical and
mental diseases.

Introduction

The lived experience of HOPE is one of feeling respected, loved, and safe. Those who share in the HOPE history do so because each was searching for relief from anguish, fear, or pain. The form of relief is individual, yet each person's words contribute to common threads of meaning.

"HOPE allows me to be me... not something I am not."

"HOPE is about optimism and solving problems and joy. It is about living with and learning from the pain."

Part One of this work presents the history of HOPE. This portion of the book includes the principles and concepts that provide structure for HOPE's framework. HOPE has experienced two decades of implementation and evolution, all the while maintaining a solid foundation from which the model operates.

HOPE's founder is a physician, Kenneth Hawley Hamilton, MD, CM, a 1960 graduate of McGill University's Faculty of Medicine, which he respects and honors for its core compassion. He retired as a surgeon to guide people on the exploration of a lifetime, that of seeking personal wisdom and life meaning. The search brings a person face-to-face with his or her ego and the attachments and attitudes that have become the ego's life partners. HOPE ever so gently invites each person to engage the ego in a new form of relationship. It does so through encouragement and the creation of a setting where release of the sometimes raw experiences of life are welcomed and respected. This safe atmosphere sets the stage from which one can examine choices and attitudes.

"It's the best thing that's ever happened to me."

"I enjoy life more than I did. It is a good place to talk about   things... to turn them around."

During 2005 Dr. Hamilton and the HOPE Board of Directors set a course to conduct a study that reflected on HOPE groups and Guides over the years. The objectives were twofold. The first was to revisit the foundations of HOPE to reflect on how these had evolved, and to determine if this model of group interaction continued to bring meaning and value to peoples' lives. The second was to create this work you hold, a tool with which to learn more about HOPE, its history, its foundation, and how to use it as a model for serving people in a variety of settings.

Part Two presents the study and its findings. These are discussed in relation to past studies of HOPE and other support groups. This most recent study was retrospective, thereby building a bridge between HOPE's rich past and the evolution to achieve its promise. The study design is primarily qualitative to reflect the nature of HOPE. The value of this framework for bringing people together in mutual support and consideration is derived from peoples' stories. The underlying principles of HOPE invite participants and Guides to welcome the gifts and challenges of each and to witness the growth that emerges along the path. Quantitative design elements include correlations based on demographic information and length and frequency of HOPE participation with level of agreement with HOPE-derived statements.

For some HOPErs the challenges arise along the thorny path associated with physical, emotional, and mental illnesses for some, and for others they arise in life's losses. In either case, as the study or stories describe, the path is about life and the revealed meaning in each day.

> "It has been an absolutely wonderful delight, honor and privilege to serve people in this way; and they have helped me appreciate my role as one who sees the value of being human." (Kenneth Hamilton, personal communication, 10/19/2006).

Part Three is subtitled "A Primer for Practitioners." People who are called to guide a HOPE group are not novices, to either life experiences or professional roles. Although a primer is an elementary book, the implication is that HOPE is an experience to which one is newly introduced. That introduction becomes part and parcel of one's journey along with relationships and encounters that contribute to the emergence of a HOPE Guide. A mature HOPE Guide is one who embodies, through heart and soul, HOPE's framework and all it represents. Quoting a HOPE Guide: "I take the work and expand it into all I do."

In this Guide's words, the work enfolds HOPE's principles, concepts, and ways of developing and renewing relationship with self and others. The expansion arises as the novice Guide opens to the awareness that one is as transformed by this work as one is an agent or witness of transformation in the lives of others.

Part Three presents the settings into which one might introduce a HOPE Group and the guidelines for doing so. The intricacies of Guide selection and preparation are offered in sufficient detail to be a resource for introductory and ongoing reflective practice. The importance of Guide selection and preparation cannot be overstated. Although the Guide is, in the deepest sense of its meaning, an active participant in the group, it is the Guide who embodies the essence of HOPE. This essence necessitates that the Guide be ever present to his/her own energy and level of wholeness. A Guide who is mature, centered, life-aware, and able to convey inner peace, solidly holds the crucible into which group members can place the fire of their lives. In the words of one whom we cherish:

"[HOPE] diminished my pain by merging it with the group's collective suffering."

Part Four is the heart of HOPE. The essence of what HOPE represents shines through in representative stories. Picture, if you will, how each reflects the light and wisdom of a hundred other stories. What each person draws from and brings to HOPE is the courage to live life fully, whether the remaining duration of that life is days or decades. This section of the book is here to inspire, to offer the refreshment of a new breath, a new way of being. On another level, it is the reunification with the soul potential that existed when each person entered this life. In the words of three of them:

"I'm alive because of it. I came alive into my own self.

"It is a place to see, connect with, and talk to people... invaluable in a time when I was so scared, depressed, and... isolated from all others."

"I became more aware of a balance in my life. I had always felt balanced but really added the importance of nature and seeing a butterfly... making those times a priority."

Part One: The History of HOPE

The Origins of HOPE

HOPE began long before the first HOPE Group meeting on February 12, 1987. It began shortly after Ken Hamilton opened his surgical practice in semi-rural Maine on January 4, 1971. One of his surgical patients asked him, in effect, if he would take the time to listen to the story of her life that she felt had an impact on her disease. He agreed, and as he listened, he realized that though he did not have answers to her questions, simply listening seemed to evoke the answers from within her. This particular kind of situation repeated itself often enough so that he became known locally as "the doctor who listens." He became recognized not so much as a counselor but as a *guide* for people in their own life travails.

Hamilton realized that a group meeting might benefit some of the people in his surgical practice who "were facing the life-threatening challenge of cancer" (Hamilton, 1996, p. 7). At the time he was dealing with his own frustrations and anger over months of experiencing several seemingly trivial, but annoyingly repetitive stresses (p.7). "I was feeling anxious, angry, lonely, and stressed out. I had hit a bottom, and was ready to change" (p. 7).

In 1975, his practice manager introduced him to the success-oriented work of the Nightingale-Conant Corporation of Niles, Illinois, sensing that this work was connected to his developing coaching/guiding skills. Hamilton (1996) was inspired by the message he heard from the co-founder, Earl Nightingale (with Lloyd Victor Conant) (Nightingale 1996) that his studies of the history of success showed that success is always related to one's attitude, and one has always chosen the current attitude, even if one has forgotten why s-he chose it in the first place. He pointed out that once a choice is made, it does not preclude change. If the old choice is not working, choose again! (p. 8)

Nightingale had begun a systematic study of success forty-three years earlier at the age of twelve, when, in the depths of the Great Depression, his father abandoned his family and young Earl saw his dreams of becoming a successful businessman fade away. However, strong determination and a passion for reading led him to embark on a study of successful people guided by the local librarian!

His studies (Nightingale, 1996) led him to define success as "the progressive realization of a worthy ideal," the authorship of which was within the ability of every human being, for each of us has such an ideal. Furthermore, Nightingale saw three keys to success: a formula found in every religious tradition, "we become what we think about most of the time"; a resource, "the mind"; and a word, "attitude" (Nightingale, 1996). Hamilton saw that he had been helping his patients recognize their "worthy ideal" by listening and encouraging them to find their own answers, and that he could guide them into selecting the most functional and effective attitudes with which to direct the efforts of their minds.

Between 1975 and 1987 Hamilton deepened his study of human development and how success and attitude mirror each other. His study of Nightingale's work "helped me greatly in bringing my own life together with meaning and sense" (Hamilton, 1996, p. 8). After ten years of working with this particular psychology and seeing the powerfully beneficial effects it had on his patients' lives and his own life, Hamilton sought guidance in counseling, and was led to receive tutoring from a gifted, complex, and wise psychiatrist in a nearby city. Through this physician, he was introduced to support groups: the self-help approach of the 12-step programs, the analytic and therapeutic support groups of Bernie Siegel, M.D., and the "attitudinal healing" support groups of Jerry Jampolsky, M.D.

Through Nightingale, Hamilton was aware of synergy, and he saw that bringing those patients with their questions into a group would increase the effectiveness and efficiency of this listening work. He invited five of his patients to come together in a supportive group on February 12, 1987. Siegel had spoken often of wanting to call his groups "H.O.P.E. Groups," but they had failed to come up with an acronym for H.O.P.E. Hamilton asked his group participants if they wanted to continue and if they wanted to call themselves a H.O.P.E. Group. In response to their affirmative reply, he asked them to figure out what the acronym stood for. At the next meeting, a week later, the nurse who was instrumental in helping him start the group offered "Healing of Persons Exceptional," which effected a firm "yes" from the group.

The group grew rapidly. Its participants talked publicly about its effectiveness, and when Christiane Northrup M.D. of nearby Falmouth, Maine, heard of it, she asked Hamilton if he would start a similar group for some of her patients. He agreed, and the second HOPE Group came into being at a teaching hospital in a nearby city. It became as effective as the first and more requests for HOPE Groups flowed in. When the fifth request came from a city two hours away, Hamilton knew that he had to choose between surgery and HOPE. The presence of two other skilled board-certified general surgeons on the staff of his hospital made it possible for him to choose HOPE and pursue his own worthy ideal of helping people heal.

When Hamilton accepted the seventh invitation to guide a local HOPE Group, which entailed driving over 600 miles a week, he knew that in order to meet any other requests, he was going to have to be able to teach people how to do the work. Others whom he trained became successful at guiding their own HOPE Groups. In 2000, with over 4000 HOPE Group meetings behind him, Hamilton backed off to guiding three HOPE Group meetings a week in order to devote time to develop the concepts and psychology further to contribute to the full development of the training/teaching methods and materials.

Today, as HOPE celebrates its twentieth anniversary, it has brought its services to over a thousand people in over 5000 HOPE Group meetings. Hamilton and HOPE's Board of Directors have been encouraged by institutions and individuals in the health care profession to bring HOPE methods and practices into the profession as an efficient venue for providing hope and care to their patients.

The Foundation and Framework of HOPE:
A derivative of contemporary cosmology.

HOPE's Philosophical precepts:

HOPE's primary core precept:

Four essential components comprise all human beings: body, mind, soul, and spirit. They are not unique to humans; rather, they are Universal; HOPE serves everyone with this belief in mind. Science knows that the quarks and electrons in our bodies have been here since the beginning of time, and, in the seeming chaos of the grand expansion, there had to have been an enfolded (implicate) order (Bohm, 2002) out of which this solar system, this planet, and all life on it arose. That order is perfect, and we are the equivalent of holographic fragments of it... perfect in that we contain its whole image. However, that image is "fuzzy" because of our relatively tiny physical size and experience; and yet we are capable of achieving ever-increasing clarity of that image because of the limitless nature of the mind.

HOPE's secondary core precept:

A human is a spiritual being whose life is the journey of a soul. The French Jesuit paleontologist Pierre Teilhard de Chardin is widely reputed to have said that we are not human beings in search of a spiritual experience, but spiritual beings immersed in the human condition. We infer from his statement that there is a spiritual director of every life, the name for which is "soul." The *Encyclopedia Britannica* 2003 CD-ROM describes soul:

> "in religion and philosophy, the immaterial aspect or essence of a human being, that which confers individuality and humanity, often considered to be synonymous with the mind or the self. In theology,

the soul is further defined as that part of the individual which partakes of divinity and often is considered to survive the death of the body."

In the experience of Raymond Moody (1992), Kenneth Ring (1984), and others contributing to the growing body of literature on near-death and out-of-body experiences, "Soul" is that which dissociates in the face of trauma. "Soul" is the focus of significant study in today's non-fiction literature, whereas twenty years ago it was absent.

We are here because Life—a fundamental property of the Universe—has created us. It has given us physical and spiritual resources with which to meet It. The physical—DNA-related and secular—resources comprise our talents and intelligences; our temperament and personality; and our will, all of which the secular director of any individual—the ego—uses to navigate its single life. The soul-related and spiritual resources consist of what Brian Tracy calls our "Core Passion" (1987). Life meets us with a set of challenging circumstances that comprise *Its* agenda. We create unique individual experiences out of that meeting. We continuously share those experiences and their associated attitudes with others. We have chosen that attitude, and Life constantly and accurately reflects it back at us. As that attitude was a choice, we have the power to make another choice, even if we can not remember why we made the original choice... and all subsequent choices of attitude.

Our ego builds its life-skills out of its experience of the interaction of its DNA-related resources with the world—both animate and inanimate—in contrast to the soul that came here knowing that it is to write another volume of experience of the Truth (that which can not be interpreted) in an encyclopedia that began lifetimes ago and will continue for lifetimes to come, resulting in a gathering of energy called experience that sustains the life of the Universe. All experience uniquely reflects the vital, changing nature of the Universe. Every one of our lives is, therefore, a unique, a one-of-a-kind work of art. We in HOPE treat each and every human being as such, asking all persons to reveal to us that which informs (Palmer, 1997) them.

Love is another fundamental property of the Universe that describes the all-inclusive relationships which describe the Universe. It is also the attitude of relationship. It is the motor of compassion and empathy. It brings us inner peace... the way to happiness.

Dialogue, as David Bohm shows us (2002), is an excellent, subjective means for sharing experience, for it reveals the order of wholeness enfolded in all apparent chaos. It works because it validates the feelings that make up the energetic thought field of the human mid-brain.

Everyone seeks an inner, spiritual essence that gives meaning to their lives. They reveal its presence in their questions and concerns about that which they see around them, most often not knowing that it is a reflection of that which lies within. At times, not aware of their quest, they reveal it in destructive behaviors. HOPE Guides do not judge these behaviors, but compassionately discern their nature, which gives them the power to listen and reflect back what they hear and feel in the presence of these seekers.

HOPE's Psychology:

Consider the lives of those with serious illness; fear, pain, uncertainty, and despair often fill their days. Consider the lives of those facing the loss of loved ones; what fills their days? Consider the lives of alcoholics; what fills their days? Consider the behavior of today's children; what fills their days? They all need the relief and salutary experience of hope, the attitude of possibility that makes it possible for individuals to rise above the *chaos of their problems* and see the enfolded *order of their possibilities* in that which has disrupted the familiar patterns of their life. A HOPE Group provides the safe environment in which to create this experience.

Hope provides us with a vitally important way to the discovery of the meaning of our lives. As Viktor Frankl tells us, hope is an "essential ingredient of the human condition." Alice Miller describes it as "a memory of the future." Indeed hope and fear both inhabit the future, where their interaction can be seen as a matter-antimatter annihilation that brings one back to the present. It follows that our choice of whether we see the future with hope or fear determines the quality of the present.

Hope is not simply a "promise of good things"; rather it is the "certainty that things can make sense, regardless of how they turn out" (Vaclav Havel). When things do not make sense, order has become chaos, and we become afraid. To Dante, in *The Divine Comedy*, hell is the place where nothing makes sense. Losing life's meaning is the source of all fear, pain, and suffering. The purpose of a HOPE Group is to support individuals while they find meaning in their lives through the examination of their suffering with the encouragement to rise above it.

People come to HOPE groups because of a wide variety of critical life situations. They may be drawn to HOPE through the hellfire of an acute illness like cancer, heart attack, or AIDS, or the black hole of a chronic condition like depression, chronic fatigue and immune dysfunction syndrome, or chronic pain. Others—the "worried well"—face their own particular hell of the risk of meaninglessness. HOPE Groups help them identify their fear and replace it with hope through the discovery of the meaning, value, and purpose in their life. Inner peace returns, and the experience of joy and happiness becomes possible, regardless of the ultimate course of the illness.

The discovery of the meaning of a life lies at the core of HOPE's psychology; "movement towards a meaningful future is not possible without viewing the past as a series of vital lessons." This psychology avoids analysis that pathologizes the past in order to create a meaningful present. Instead, it asks each of us to view the past as an integrated, molding, and shaping experience that challenges us to find meaning, value, and purpose in our present lives.

All of our problems arise from the way in which the ego looks at life—though the lens of fear. The possibilities of our lives lie in the solutions to the problems, which can only take place through the nature of the soul to examine life through the lens of love. HOPE perceives that our significant problems almost invariably arose in childhood during the tender time of ego-development, so the solution lies in rising to the level of one's "higher self"–the soul–the Ancient Greek name of which is Psyche. Indeed, the word, psychology, literally means "soul study."

To examine any life through the lens of love is to bring compassion into it, and thus forgiveness becomes possible. To fail to forgive is to remain attached to the suffering of the situation. At this level, the fundamental chemical energies of the adrenals–adrenalin and cortisol–rule the internal environment of the body with toxic effects on the heart and the immune system. At this level, the problem can only perpetuate itself. Through forgiveness and compassion, the energy level of the body rises out of the survival response through courage to wisdom and, ultimately, to serenity–inner peace.

It is the function of a HOPE Group and its Guide to focus on what is possible and thus to rise into this higher, creative state of function in which the possibilities offered by the situation manifest themselves. This creative state is the essence of success as defined by Earl Nightingale. Implied in this comprehensive description is process and value that result in service, "the rewards of which are always in direct proportion to the level and degree of that service" (Hill, 1937).

Furthermore, any study of humans reveals the stunning fact that no two are alike, not even identical twins. Indeed we are all *exceptional* and yet we are all *persons* with our species' collective knowledge—our field of consciousness that gives rise to our form—the *morphic field* of Rupert Sheldrake (1998). As Cheri Huber put it a decade ago,

> "Yes, I am me, but what animates me is what
> animates Uncle Bob, the cat, the tree, the rock and
> all that is. We are packaged differently, but we share

the same essence. There are many of us and we are not the same but we are all one" (personal communication).

And HOPE does its work by acknowledging and validating the many and the one and their varied and marvelous passions, dreams, and intentions.

Principles of HOPE Group Function:

Loving kindness—compassion—is the motor of this psychology; forgiveness leading to inner peace and, ultimately, to happiness, is the consequence. HOPE Guides know that we must acknowledge the past in order to forgive judgments about it that paralyze both our present and future growth. They appreciate the value of the popular perception about anger... it is like taking poison and expecting the object of the anger to die. They appreciate that forgiveness—completely giving away attachments—is possible only where love and compassion prevail. HOPE Guides provide people with a compassionate, soft-eyed approach to their lives. They encourage people to see themselves as beings called to life by Life itself that has provided them with a set of personal resources with which to meet the unique circumstances that Life gives them. HOPE Guides encourage people to believe in themselves as spiritual beings with the power to use their resources and circumstances to transform their lives into meaningful blessing-gifts to themselves, to their fellow human beings, and to Life itself.

HOPE Guiding seeks clarity of feelings, thoughts, and actions.

HOPE Groups are gatherings of people who come together to find wellness by replacing fear with hope, the key to deepening the meaning, value, and purpose of their lives, and love, the relationship-centered context of all healing. In short, they are catalysts of change; they help people appreciate that all action proceeds out of thought, and all thought is subject to the effects of attitudes—feelings. HOPE Guides provide this supportive service for people who want to move forward in their lives, either by getting through a crisis or by progressing to the next level of personal development. HOPE Guides do not pretend to be able to heal; rather they work to help people discover their own healing powers themselves. Thus HOPE Groups evoke strengths that increase the possibilities that exist within each one of us for living a creative life, and they focus on bringing that life into its creativity.

HOPE Groups are not conventional therapy groups.

HOPE Groups differ from traditional therapeutic groups in that they do not seek to diagnose or prescribe specific treatments for what is "wrong." They do not seek to decrease symptoms of mental and physical health problems; though such results are common benefits of HOPE Group participation. HOPE Groups also differ from traditional "support" groups in that they do not "support" a problem by using its label, e.g. cancer, alcoholism, anxiety, depression, chronic pain; rather, HOPE groups acknowledge the value of having good support in understanding the problem and guiding a person to focus on the meaning and possibilities that life contains and on that which lies beyond the problem—to discover the personal resources that enable them to rise above the problem to discover its possibilities and, therefore, its solution.

HOPE Groups are resources of shared individual experiences in living life through all of its challenges and rewards. Participating in one is an opportunity for the individual participant to discover their life's intention... to choose how they want to realize that intention... on their own timetable and on their own unique path. HOPE Groups use *The Gold Book*, a four-page, 5.5 x 8.5 inch laminated document which sets the *context* for the meeting with the prime directive: "We come together to find the wellness that comes with the discovery of peace of mind," discovering the attitudes that influence that achievement, and a verbal contract of meeting conduct and responsibilities. In this way, group participants create for themselves the agenda for each meeting.

HOPE Group Guides' primary responsibilities to the group are fourfold: First, to help with great gentleness, without taking root in someone else's mind (BKWSU). Second, to hold the group to the context set by sharing *The Gold Book,* and to model active listening by reflecting back to the speaker what they have heard. Third, to affirm the presence of movement and direction aligned to a personal intention. Fourth, to trust the sought-after answers that arise from within the person with the question or concern.

HOPE Groups and their relation to the goals of medicine.

Eric J. Cassell, M.D., begins and ends his book, *The Nature of Suffering and the Goals of Medicine* (Cassell, 2004), with the idea that the fundamental role of medicine is the relief of suffering. In light of today's emphasis on the use of science and technique in the practice of medicine, both of which are of vital importance for the medical profession's effectiveness, and the pressures of practicing medicine according to managed-care standards, the relief of suffering is seen as "too soft" and time-consuming.

The diagnosis and treatment of a disease is, most certainly, an essential responsibility of all physicians. However, as Cassell points out with rich thoroughness, the physician must also discover and relate to the *person* in whom the disease exists. This discovery has always been a primary function of HOPE Groups. While science is a method of measurement, replication, and prediction that results in the establishment of *absolute* facts—here, diseases—the individual human being—the person—is a unique *particular* that is scientifically indescribable. Medicine, in order to alleviate suffering must practice bringing the absolutes to the particulars—the science to the individual person. HOPE Groups help here by recognizing and acknowledging that no two of us are alike; thus they help individual persons discover those resources with which they have met the vicissitudes of life and use them in the current situation. A HOPE Group helps people discover how to convey their individual—personal—needs to their families, their friends, and their physicians.

Furthermore, HOPE Groups create a highly efficient opportunity for creative therapeutic interaction of science and technology and the uniquely individual person.... Twelve people meeting in a synergistically supportive HOPE Group for two hours averages out to ten minutes for each patient!

HOPE Guiding holds integrity.

HOPE groups are places where people explore *who* they are, not *what* they have, *what* they have done, or *what* others think of them, which includes their labels—their diagnoses and prognoses. They learn to see life as a call from Life, itself—a blessing. They learn to see that Life has met them with a set of circumstances that may well have contained a heartbreak, and how they see that breaking determines the quality of the gift that they have to give life in return for that life. They do so by asking four questions that evoke meaning: "Who are you?" "Why are you here?" "How are you going to get what you came for?" "What are you going to do with it when you have it?" Thus, they demonstrate the power of integrity so well described in Shakespeare's mandate, "This above all: to thine own self be true, and it must follow, as the night the day, thou canst not then be false to any man." (Polonius, in *Hamlet*)

HOPE groups build a safe context within which the answers to those questions can evolve of their own natural accord. HOPE groups have simple "Guidelines" of behavior that sustain the safety of the environment. Some people who run volunteer-facilitated groups have suggested that these questions are "therapy" and they belong in licensed, certified, "degreed" practices, to which we reply that these questions come out of the public (read "non-therapeutic") domain and not from any standard texts of psychology or psychotherapy. Hamilton's work of the past thirty years has all grown out of this public domain and is focused on success (Earl Nightingale's worthy ideal). HOPE would offer the potential to develop these evocative skills to the facilitators of any of this nation's thousands of self-help groups.

Most people need a HOPE Group from time to time.

The need to participate in a HOPE group exists in almost every one of us at some time or another. Most of us seek the support of a group when a serious disease confronts us, such as cancer, AIDS, depression, or alcoholism. Some come with less "serious" conditions such as chronic fatigue syndrome, emphysema, arthritis, or lupus. Some come with depression, bipolar, or anxiety disorders. For some, life just isn't going the way they want. For some, it is essential that their fellow group participants have conditions similar to theirs. For others, open, eclectic groups are appropriate. HOPE does not argue these points; it merely seeks to respond to the wishes of each group, and encourage forward movement of the group. HOPE's belief and experience is that there is a way for each of us through the difficulties of disease to the discovery of health.

A HOPE Guide has a specific function.

The function of a HOPE Guide is to look at each life as a rich, though sometimes painful, yet always challenging, experience. The Guide helps the participant to see how that rich experience can direct a life towards the discovery of its own meaning. The Guide's purpose is not to analyze a life or to help people find specific goals in their life, but to follow the leadings of this psychology. HOPE Guides bridge the past and the future by focusing on living in the present moment–the "now" moment of J. Krishnamurti and as skillfully developed by Eckhart Tolle (2001).

HOPE Group Concepts:

HOPE Group Method: "guiding".

We do not consider that HOPE Guides be "facilitators." Their work is not to make easy the seeker's path. We do not believe that we follow a path that another has laid out for us. Rather, we are finding our way across a pathless land, and can benefit from hearing other people's experiences with their paths. We are students and teachers to each other. In this way we learn to identify potential pitfalls and pratfalls on our own paths. A HOPE Guide discourages advice giving, criticism, and judgment and encourages the sharing of experience in an atmosphere of respect and confidentiality. In *volunteer* HOPE Groups, the Guides do not keep written notes or records of any individual with whom they are working in the group. In *professional* HOPE Groups, the professionals are bound by the ethical confidentiality standards of their professions and they do enter information into the individuals' clinical records to help in the management of their therapies.

All HOPE Guides work with clarity of intent and purpose and follow the context of *The Gold Book* that acknowledges past experiences, validates present life, and helps their fellow human beings to recognize and describe their potential. It then encourages them to reach out for it. All HOPE Guides focus on attitudinal shifts that transform an individual's guilty and/or shameful *reactions* to a traumatic set of circumstances into healthy *responses*. They guide individuals towards focusing on and setting and clarifying intentions, and developing and implementing initiatives. The process moves people forward toward appreciating the secular and finite ego's disappointment, resentment, anger or bitterness with a situation and turning it over to the spiritual director of life, the soul, who knows the greater meaning and value of the situation—who rises above the situation that binds the ego.

HOPE Guides recognize that emotions and attitudes are intimately connected and have a profound subconscious effect on the life of every individual. In this way, HOPE Guides work with people to create attitudinal shifts that transform harmful responses based on the dark triad of guilt, fear, and anger into the beneficial responses of hope, love, and peace. Accordingly, we come to identify with the order that created our Universe. HOPE Guides also recognize the power of the dark triad to overwhelm people and are readily prepared to advise them to seek professional help in such situations to augment their recovery program.

HOPE Guides encourage the use of subjective "I" statements that are personal, experiential, and other-serving. They discourage the use of objective "you" statements that are impersonal, instructing, advising, and self-serving. They critique behaviors rather than judge personalities. They are active listeners who safeguard the health of all participants. And, of greatest importance, HOPE Guides actively encourage the compassionate sharing of experiences of life.

HOPE Guides help people construct and reconstruct their lives:

They help people focus on that which makes them feel whole, integrated and healthy—an attitudinal belief that things can make sense (Vaclav Havel) and gives life meaning (Victor Frankl). This process helps people recognize old labels with which they identified themselves and create new, honest, and realistic descriptions, which help them shift their state of mind from illness toward wellness, both of which are *states of being mindsets.* It encourages them to live in the present moment, free of projections and attachments and to focus on the whole of life rather than the fragments. It also encourages them to see that they are the sum total of all the choices they have made in their lives and that they can choose again and rewrite their story in any way that they wish. It encourages them to use the two attitudes that Victor Frankl found common to all concentration camp survivors—hope and love—and use them to focus on developing a life story that contains a worthy ideal—the very essence of success.

HOPE groups as non-therapy:

All HOPE groups are powerful forms of what is currently called "cognitive restructuring" that in reality follow centuries-old principles of creating and living successful lives by "reframing" hindrances into opportunities, and problems into possibilities.

Volunteer HOPE guides are not expected to practice any form of therapy in their open, on-going HOPE Groups. They are not there to treat members' diseases. They encourage anyone needing conventional therapy to find it outside the group.

HOPE Groups as clinical services:

Professionally guided, clinical HOPE Groups provide a safe environment in which the participants can explore the qualities of their relationships with their healthcare professionals. They provide a healthy, safe forum for discussing the effects of the individual participant's therapies.

Professional HOPE Groups guided by HOPE-trained professionals (nurses, nurse practitioners, physician assistants, and physicians) provide valuable information about their individual therapies that help their healthcare providers make beneficial therapeutic decisions.

In their invitation to find meaning in life, professional HOPE Groups provide a safe venue for the (re-) implementation of the placebo effect on all therapies.

HOPE Guiding comprises five simple elements that define the operating system:

1. Listening with open heart and mind;
2. Asking open, honest questions for clarification and deeper understanding;
3. Avoiding criticizing or advice-giving;
4. Affirming people for their experience of the way in which they have met life's circumstances; and
5. Encouraging them to create benefit for self and others from that experience.

HOPE Guiding avoids the use of the pathological assumption and questions:

"What's broke?"
"What caused it?"
"What can we do to fix it?"

Instead, it prefers questions that ask for the story of the individuals' experiences of life, how they have met it in the past, how they would like to meet it in both the present and the future, and how they will feel when they know they have succeeded. Thus, HOPE's evocative psychology and related HOPE Guide work complement virtually all forms of counseling, psychotherapy, coaching, and self-help groups.

Requirements to be a HOPE Guide:

General:

HOPE Guiding requires mature-for-age, caring, healthy people who have no active, debilitating disease and who have the ability and desire to listen to others with discernment and compassion, reflect on what they have just heard, convey their reflections, encourage others to use their personal resources to meet the circumstances of their lives, and affirm them for every step in the process. HOPE guides do not seek to change people, but delight in seeing them evolve, which is a natural and divine function of human life. HOPE guides follow the precept: "If you have come here to help me, you are wasting your time. But if you have come because your liberation is tied up with mine, then let us work together." (Lilla Watson, Aboriginal activist). HOPE Guides come from all occupations—including psychotherapists, counselors, and coaches who leave their therapies at the door when they come to do HOPE work—working to ease the human travail by sharing their liberation in a safe place.

Specific for all HOPE Groups:

Every HOPE Guide has met certain requirements:

- Has participated in a SoulCircling exercise and HOPE group meetings.
- Has submitted to HOPE an application consisting of a HOPE resume ("a description of those personal resources with which they met life, the circumstances that life met them with,

the experiences they have created out of the interaction including education and work, and their intention for becoming a HOPE group guide"), and writing a review of Viktor Frankl's book, *Man's Search for Meaning*.

- Has read and become familiar with *SoulCircling: The Journey to the Who*, and *The HOPE Guide's Manual*.
- Has participated in Level 1 HOPE Group Guide training.
- Has made a conscious decision to replace the conventional mechanical/industrial model questions mentioned above.
- Has agreed to ask for the story of the individual's experience of life, how they met it in the past, and how they want to meet it in the future... in short, life-affirming questions, rich in potential.
- Has agreed to validate the uniqueness of an individual's experience as a way through the pathless land of truth to the essence of life—love.

Specific for HOPE Groups in clinical services:

The HOPE Guide of a clinical service HOPE Group must be a licensed professional who is employed by and familiar with the exact nature of the therapies offered by that service. This person is qualified by that service to be familiar with the patients' clinical records and able to make additions to those records with the full knowledge and consent of the participating patients. Such persons would be subject to all ethical and legal standards of their licensure.

Relationships with health and Health Care.

Health

To begin with, the root word for health is also the root word for heal, whole, holistic, and holy. This root makes it impossible for health to be defined in terms of disease, as in "health is the absence of disease". Health's implication of wholeness and holiness makes it possible to define disease as the absence of health.

It is a current standard to define a whole, healthy human being as comprised of three parts: body, mind, and spirit. However, at this time in our evolution, it is important to recognize the fact that prior to the Age of Reason in the early part of the 17th century, a "whole" human being comprised body, mind, *soul,* and spirit. The Scientific Age had just begun, and the rule for validation of any natural phenomenon was scientific proof. "Scientific proof" needed to be able to analyze a phenomenon and replicate it in order for that phenomenon to be predictable and, therefore, real. The soul failed this test, thus it was determined that the soul could not exist. Ironically, the most outstanding figure of the Age of Reason, René Descartes, wrote a carefully crafted piece at the very end of his life called "The Passions of the Soul," in which he meticulously placed the soul deep within the brain in the pineal gland. In this way, he preserved it until a more evolved science could begin to describe it in the 21st century.

Today, there are hundreds of nonfiction books in print whose topic is the soul, the properties of which are well described in the citation in the Encyclopedia Britannica. Because of this genuine interest in the soul, which would seem to be the equivalent of the "higher Self" of many spiritual traditions, and, therefore, a spiritual guide or director of life, it would seem to contrast powerfully to the secular director of life, the "self" or ego. It would seem appropriate to restore the soul to its component place in human nature and consider that in order to study the soul, we must create new scientific hypotheses that lend themselves to its measurement and replication.

Health Care

When the United States government got involved in reimbursement for medical and surgical services in 1966, it created new titles for the professional and the patient: "health care provider" and "health care consumer," respectively. It was certainly a shock to some professionals to discover that they were no longer professionals in disease care, for which they had been rigorously and meticulously educated and trained but had somehow become experts in health care... overnight. The persistent use of the term, "healthcare," suggests that the time has come for the healthcare professions to truly *care* for the *health* of those whom they serve.

Getting the government involved in health care to such a degree indicates how much health care has become an industry. Consequently, health care was effectively told that it must abrogate its responsibilities to serve society as a healer and focus instead upon scientific and technical approaches to disease management. Ironically, this made it virtually impossible for health care to care for the health of those whom it served. Medical professionals, the majority of whom saw themselves as healers when they entered medical school, object more and more today to such constraints. Jerome E. Groopman, M.D., makes this perfectly clear (Pories, Jain, & Harper, 2006, p.xiii):

> "Certainly the primary imperative of a physician is to be skilled in medical science, but if he or she does not probe a patient's soul, then the doctor's care is given without caring, and part of the sacred mission of healing is missing."

This also a major thesis in Cassell's work (2004).

HOPE Groups are safe places in which persons can expose their souls to the care and nurturance of the meeting. Whether they manifest as volunteer or professional groups, these groups fit the current business model for cost effectiveness, and, at the same time, they nurture and heal those whom they serve.

In summary:

"HOPE is spiritual. HOPE Groups and SoulCircling are sacred processes. It cuts through all that is superficial. Engaging in HOPE eliminates all pretenses. This is what you call an 'open heart'. No where else does this happen with such regularity."
   Colleen R.

Quote references in support of HOPE's views of the past.

"All of us, whether guilty or not, whether old or young, must accept the past. It is not a case of coming to terms with the past. That is not possible. It cannot be subsequently modified or undone."   ~Richard von Weizsäcker

"Those who cannot remember the past are condemned to repeat it."   ~George Santayana

"The present contains nothing more than the past, and what is found in the effect was already in the cause." ~Henri Bergson

"To look back to antiquity is one thing, to go back to it is another."   ~Charles Caleb Colton

"Some are so very studious of learning what was done by the ancients that they know not how to live with the moderns."
~William Penn

"So that we may move on in life, it is not that we should forgive and forget; rather it is that we must forgive and remember. Thus we free ourselves from our past conditioning."
~Ken Hamilton

Part Two: HOPE Group and Guide Study Project

Study Purpose

The HOPE Group and Guide Study Project was designed to gather information about the factors that distinguish HOPE Groups among supportive groups. Support groups have been a research focus for the last two decades (Arthur & Edwards, 2005; Zabalegui, Sanchez, Sanchez, & Juando, 2005). Support group studies have emerged from the science of addictions (Brown, Whitney, Schneider, & Vega, 2006), and investigations of interventions for care of people with cancer (Coward, 2005; Grande, Myers, & Sutton, 2005; Ziegler, Smith, & Fawcett, 2004), chronic pain (Arthur & Edwards, 2005), trauma (Knight, 2006) or emotional-behavioral issues (Dadich, 2006; Ruffolo, Kuhn, & Evans, 2006). Support group research may focus on a particular disease, potentially limiting the support group participant's perspective to the illness-related experience (Dadich, 2006; Knight, 2006).

Information that was gathered from this study will be integrated with previously written HOPE materials to prepare a manual for practice. The foundation of attitudinal healing serves as the theoretical framework for the conduct of this inquiry. This framework aligns with a holistic worldview in which the overlap of theories deepens life understanding and invites fresh insights to bring to the human experience (Capra, 1996). The HOPE Group Study tested these hypotheses:

1. HOPE Groups promote an awareness of wholeness that guides people to move from fear and fragmentation to love and unity.
2. The HOPE Guide's presence and conduct directly influence the lived experience of HOPE Group participants.

Review of the Literature

A review of the literature was conducted for several purposes associated with this study. The first was to gather information to further inform the process of retrospective reflection of HOPE Groups and Guides. The second was to gather information from the support group literature to contribute to HOPE Group training material preparation in anticipation of expansion into clinical settings. Lastly, the literature was surveyed to examine how the HOPE Group and Guide Project might contribute to the understanding of support groups.

Searches were conducted using the Cumulative Index of Nursing and Allied Health Literature (CINAHL) and PsycINFO. Rationale for use of these databases includes projections that nurses and allied health professionals, as well as physicians, will guide HOPE Groups in clinical service settings. The six Guides, aside from Hamilton, who were interviewed as part of this study, come from the disciplines of education, psychology, health care administration, and retail marketing.

Database searches focused on support groups and associated topics such as facilitator training and research. These content areas are relevant to the understanding of HOPE's knowledge about who will attend and participate in groups, and benefit from the experience of viewing life from another person's perspective. Basic searches that limited the term to 'support groups' yielded more results than did expanded options. A literature review and meta-analysis were included in this selection because of the depth of knowledge each added to the understanding of the HOPE framework and insights that would potentially contribute to Guide selection and professional development. Lessons from this mixed review may serve to guide the design of HOPE training materials, integration into clinical settings, and future studies.

One of the more interesting challenges to reviewing the literature in relation to a support group such as HOPE, was that it is an open group that consciously focuses on the person and the life experience rather than on disease and the support group as a disease-specific intervention. Studies that either examined or recommended the use of support groups as an intervention for health-related issues, included those with a focus on breast cancer (Coward, 2005; Zeigler et al., 2004), cardiac disease (Paquet, Bolduc, Xhignesse, & Vanasse, 2005) and social emotional needs (Dadich, 2006; Knight, 2006; Leung & Arthur, 2004).

All but one of the studies that were part of this review were published between 2002 and 2006; the exception was published in 1998. The literature review and meta-analysis that are part of this review studied support group research from the last 25 years. People from around the world are discovering that group support provides a community in which a person can retain or strengthen a sense of self while living with illness. Ten authors from outside the United States wrote articles included in this review. Countries of origin include the United Kingdom, Canada, Australia, Denmark, Spain, Hong Kong, and Finland.

This review of the literature included groups with a self-help structure, others that were community-based with a professional facilitator, and some that were part of a clinical health care setting. Seventeen studies focused on people who belonged to groups for those with a specific diagnosis or illness. Of the whole, eight (40%) focused on people with cancer and seven focused on people with mental health/emotional/behavioral needs. The remaining articles focused on cardiac disease, HIV, and aging. Two articles focused on learning more about approaches to reach and serve people in the future, suggesting increased support group availability.

This review illuminated several factors to consider when planning for and implementing support groups. Group participants reported that a feeling of safety within the group experience permits emotional sharing. This sharing was expressed as beyond that done with families and intimates in order to spare loved ones added pain and anguish (Adamsen & Rasmussen, 2003). The support group experience reduces the sense of social isolation that people with mental health and trauma can experience (Dadich, 2006; Knight, 2006). Current medical and psychotherapeutic settings do not meet all of peoples' needs, particularly as they deal with life-altering health changes and long-term sequelae (Paquet, et al., 2005). Support groups, because of their value to participants and contribution to seamless, cost-effective care (Zabalegui, et al., 2005), emerged as a method suggested to provide people with help that is not currently part of medical and psychotherapeutic intervention in numerous settings (Arthur & Edwards, 2005; Vivar &McQueen, 2005; Ziegler, et al., 2004;). Improved quality of life was revealed to be a statistically significant outcome of support group intervention in the meta-analysis of studies that investigated their effect on those living with cancer, whereas increase in life span was not (Zabalegui, et al., 2005). A number of studies within this review, all published in peer-reviewed international and U.S. health care journals, relied on qualitative forms of data collection and analysis to conduct research (Adamsen & Rasmussen, 2003; Dadich, 2006; Leung & Arthur, 2004; Paquet et al., 2005; Ziegler et al., 2004). Of the twenty studies reviewed, several focused on the guides' or facilitators' group participation preparation or experience (Adamsen & Rasmussen, 2003; Knight, 2006; Leung & Arthur, 2004; Pitkala et. al, 2004; Ziegler et. al, 2004).

The initial intent of this review was to gather support group information that would contribute to the retrospective nature, and subsequent discussion, of the HOPE Study and its findings. It was anticipated that the search would yield comparative demographic data and research design methods to contribute to future prospective studies, as well as material that would enrich Guide training materials. What resulted, in part because of this review, was the heightened realization that HOPE has stood the test of time as a support group model. Further, its foundations and philosophy fulfill many of the recommendations suggested for support group theory and implementation.

Findings of Past HOPE Studies

Three studies have been conducted in the past on behalf of H.O.P.E. Brophy, Skillings, and Chandler (1991) conducted a community assessment of HOPE as part of graduate nursing studies at the University of Southern Maine. Tatton (1997), a graduate social work student at another university located in Maine, gathered information to answer the question "What do the members think about HOPE groups?" (p. 1). The HOPE Board of Directors approved a third study that was conducted in 1998 to "better understand the impact of HOPE's training programs and improve the service we give to future trainees" (p. 1).

HOPE participants (n=38) in 1991 (Brophy, Skillings, & Chandler) reported that 24% were referred to HOPE by their physician, 24% did self-referral for emotional reasons, 24% referred self for physical reasons, and 13% participated to support a friend. The remaining 15% (5% for each) were evenly distributed in participation to support a spouse, being referred by someone else, or volunteering (p. 9). The respondents stated they had learned about the HOPE group through the HOPE newsletter (31%), via word of mouth (22%), from their physician (22%), directly from Dr. Hamilton (17%), or from other sources (8%). Length of HOPE involvement for people in this study was: 32% up to one year, 16% one year, 26% two years, 21% three years, and 5% four years.

Educational level of the participants in the 1991 study (Brophy, Skillings, & Chandler, p. 10), were 58% with a high school diploma or bachelor's degree; 15.4% with a graduate degree; and, 10.3% who did not complete high school. Gender distribution was reported to be 68% female and 32% male. Subjects in this sample ranged from 30 years to over 70 years, with no distribution data reported.

Group size in South Paris at the time of the 1991 study (Brophy, Skillings, and Chandler) ranged between four and twenty-five. The interaction and conversation during these meetings focused on feelings and attitudes, with Hamilton asking questions in order for a person to draw her/his own conclusions. "The conversation isn't so much directed toward the physical ailment that is bothering the person but how the whole process is shaping his/her attitudes" (p. 5).

Sixty-nine percent of the people who participated in the 1991 study (Brophy, Skillings, and Chandler) derived benefit from the emotional support and proactive attitude present during a HOPE meeting, with the remaining 31% reporting overall benefit from the meetings, including those who were in the role of guide (6%). Subjects were asked to report on what ways HOPE least benefited them; most left this blank, with minimal responses about group challenges or no longer needing the group. This study did not report on physical healing of participants because there was a lack of data. Those who reported on the illness they were experiencing fell into the following disease clusters: cardiovascular disease, degenerative disorders, cancers, depression, gastrointestinal disease, and addictions.

Conclusions of the Brophy, Skillings, and Chandler study (1991) regarding HOPE as a framework and method of providing group support include: demonstration of "a positive approach to health and health promotion, the appearance of positive trends of healing among participants according to subjective accounts, and "it has appeared to deepen the quality of lives of the patients" (p. 17).

The 1997 member survey (Tatton) was mailed to 241 current or former HOPE group members. Sixty-seven surveys were returned, representing a 28% survey response rate. This study was designed to determine what HOPE members thought of the groups. Methodology was qualitative; peoples' comments were gathered and subjected to content analysis. Demographic data were not part of the report that was accessible to this author.

The largest numbers of responses (n=45) were those that reflected the "safety and supportiveness of the groups" (Tatton, 1997, p. 1). Examples of those included in this cluster are:

"Many of us had the same problems. It was very close."

"There was a positive atmosphere. There was honor, respect, and caring."

Fourteen comments were directed to the value of information sharing that occurred during meetings. Four comments expressed confidence in the Guide's skills, three suggested the helpfulness of attitudinal healing, and three "found the format of the group helpful" (p. 2). Four people indicated that they valued imagery and relaxation exercises during the meeting and four members had favorable comments regarding group size and location.

Criticisms expressed in response to the question "what do you like least?" included eight comments about group size and distance, eight about tangential conversations, and seven from people who had difficulty relating to other peoples' issues. Other content areas and number of associated comments included miscellaneous dislikes (n=6), painful feelings (n=5), conflicts with the guide (n=5), changes in group membership (n=3), and group size (n=3) (Tatton, 1997, p. 3).

Lastly, members were asked to respond to the question "Is there anything that could make the HOPE group more helpful to you? If so, what do you think that might be?" (Tatton, 1997, p. 5). Results were clustered into the following categories, represented here with the number of suggestions for each: stronger recruitment and advertising (n=7), more structure in the groups (n=7), more direction from the guide (n=6), start new groups (n=4), more information sharing (n=3), specialized groups (n=2), replacement guides (n= 2), and more guided imagery (n=2).

Tatton's (1997) findings and recommendations follow his observation "not everyone is going to be satisfied all the time, nor can HOPE groups meet all the members' needs. But if two or more people are saying the same thing, it may be suspected that the feeling is shared by others" (p. 6). Recommendations were summarized in the content areas of recruitment, creation of voice options, membership, and training. Recruitment was briefly presented as the function of attracting members to extend the reach and health of groups. The suggestion to conduct periodic member surveys was to assure that "group discussions are on track" or to check in on how people felt the group was functioning (p. 7). "In order to stay healthy groups should periodically take stock of themselves" (p. 7).

One recommendation to stimulate group involvement was to create opportunities to "connect them [members] more organically with the group" (p. 7). Tatton's (1997) observation was that those attending the group may see it as the Guide's responsibility to address issues such as attendance.

"The results of the survey indicate that HOPE groups are quite successful in creating a safe and supportive place for people to work on healing" (Tatton, 1997, p. 7). Training recommendations were derived from the findings that offered suggestions for ways to maintain a safe and supportive environment through a Guide's "attention to keep group members to the HOPE group guidelines" (p. 7). Additional training suggestions presented within this study were information about group development, the nature of group dynamics, and methods for guiding emerging patterns.

H.O.P.E.'s (1998) Board of Directors requested a study to survey the opinions of HOPE Guides, Guide trainees, and Circling the Soul (now called SoulCircling) participants. Responses (n=29) included information related to the HOPE training's effect on one's life, with whom people were sharing HOPE's message, how HOPE training lessons have been transformed into action, and other information to share with the HOPE organization. "Of the 29 returned, 75% had participated in a *Circling the Soul: Coming Home to Yourself*™ or *Art and Soul of Healing* workshop, 66% were or had been a participant in a HOPE Group, 41% had received Introduction to HOPE Guide Training, 41% had received HOPE Guide Level I training, 10% had received HOPE Guide Level II training, and 24% were or had been HOPE Group Guides" (HOPE, 1998, p. 1).

The majority of respondents shared favorable comments when asked how the HOPE training had most affected her/his life. These included "applicable to daily life," "connected and open to who I really am," "given my life direction," and "releasing addictive and non-productive patterns" (HOPE, 1998, p.1). In response to questioning whom people were touching with HOPE's message, people noted family, friends, and others with whom they had contact. HOPE Guides and those in the helping professions reported use of the HOPE principles with clients and group members.

The response theme of "professional as well as personal use of HOPE training skills" carried over to the replies when asked how HOPE training workshop lessons had been translated into life action (HOPE, 1998, p. 2). Professional action included use of HOPE principles with work in the mental health field and a complementary care practice. Two other professionally associated responses included one person who wanted to start a HOPE group and another who wanted to find a full-time purpose for the HOPE training. "Personally participants...use HOPE principles to 'keep me going when things were difficult' and to 'repeatedly use attitude shift [and] reframing'" (p. 2).

A request for other information that respondents wished to share about the HOPE training experience ranged from expressions of gratitude for Ken's influence and caring to being "thankful to find a program that was not pushing medication to cover symptoms, but a process of finding HOPE in one's life" (HOPE, 1998, p. 2). Suggestions included regular Guide meetings and a "supervised practice field" in which participants could "examine what their motivation is for doing this work as we can only guide to the point of our own health" (p. 2).

Less favorable responses to the topics noted above were reported as being few. These included not understanding the training or its application, not having used HOPE's lessons in one's life, "struggling to find a purpose to my life," and having negative perceptions about a Circling the Soul session (HOPE, 1998, p. 2).

Twenty people (69%) reported that they used HOPE skills in their occupation. "Professions listed ranged from architect to ship builder, to court secretary to speech pathologist, to teachers, nurses, and mental health counselors, social workers, and healers" (HOPE, 1998, p. 3). One person stated that because of HOPE "I help them see possibilities and not expectations" and its use is "very integrated into my approach." Another felt "I am a catalyst for supporting individuals to focus on love, their talents/gifts and what is right" (p.3).

Methodology

Study design was reviewed and approved by the Board of Directors of H.O.P.E., Incorporated, a 501(C)(3) organization located in South Paris, Maine. The board approved privacy assurances associated with this study that included: a private consultant conduct the study with secure document storage capacity and coding of study materials that assure confidentiality.

Subjects for this study were a purposive sample of HOPE Group participants and Guides; the subjects have either present or past involvement with HOPE. Participants were recruited with the assistance of Kenneth Hamilton, M.D., the founder and principal of HOPE.

This retrospective, descriptive correlational study was non-experimental and used mixed methods for data collection and analysis. The study relied on qualitative data collection methods supported by quantitative information. Qualitative methods included group observations and participant and Guide interviews. Two questionnaires collected data that measured level of agreement with statements derived from HOPE Group materials and a limited amount of demographic information. Study methodology included data collection that permitted examination of correlations that potentially existed between descriptive data and measured opinions.

Data Collection and Management

Quantitative data collection methods surveyed basic demographic information, including gender, age range, county of residence, and educational level. This same questionnaire, as seen in Appendix A, asked participants to share which HOPE group or groups they had attended, their dates of attendance, and an approximate number of meetings they had attended. These data were analyzed using SPSS for Windows, Version 11.0. The study design for the quantitative analysis was descriptive correlational, seeking to establish if correlations existed between descriptive data and level of agreement with HOPE-derived statements.

The level of agreement questionnaire, as displayed in Appendix B, requested that participants and Guides select a level of agreement with 15 statements that were extracted from or based on HOPE literature, such as *The Gold Book* (Hamilton, 1993). Questionnaire design used a four-point Likert scale to force choice and eliminate responses that might fall into an undecided category (Burns & Grove, 2001). Values for level of agreement with each statement were based on scoring with '1' indicating a level of 'strongly disagree' to '4' a level of 'strongly agree.' Three of the statements were negatively expressed to alter the potential for bias. Ten statements were participant-focused, measuring each person's present state of mind and being regarding HOPE. Five statements were Guide-focused with the purpose of ascertaining how each person perceived the Guide's conduct and presence during the meeting. Results from the level of agreement questionnaire were entered into and analyzed by use of SPSS for Windows, Version 11.0, using the methods described above.

Phenomenological collection methods included group observations, participant and Guide interviews, and one focus group with Guides. These methods supported the acquisition of further understanding of HOPE Group Principles, Guides' perceptions of support and benefits derived from HOPE Group participation, and the influence of a HOPE Group Guide's presence and conduct on group function and outcomes.

The study design planned for group observations to occur in two locations, with the option for supplemental observations in a third location. Each group was to be observed for the two-hour duration of six meetings. The study's nurse consultant conducted the observations based on guidelines developed from suggested group conduct as described by Hamilton (1996) in *The HOPE Guide's Manual*, and depicted in Appendix C.

Group participants were informed about the study prior to an observation's occurrence. On the first day of a group's observation, the nurse consultant introduced herself and provided group participants with a study packet that included a consent form, two questionnaires (Appendixes A and B), and a copy of the participant interview guidelines (Appendix D). Participants were invited to complete and return the documents when convenient for them to do so. The observer described the process of the study and requested that people who did not wish to have their words transcribed state their wishes. In such cases the observer refrained from writing that person's portions of the dialogue.

The consultant transcribed each person's words to paper. A select number, based on where s/he sat in the circle, identified each person. Thus each person might have a different number, week to week. Meeting transcriptions were word processed and saved for analysis and storage.

The study design planned for up to forty interviews to be conducted with present and past HOPE participants and Guides. Interview methodology described here applied to both group participants and Guides. Each interviewee was provided with the study packet described above and a time was selected for the interview based on what fit within each person's schedule. It was anticipated that most interviews would be conducted by phone with opportunity provided for a face-to-face experience for those people who preferred that option. A minimum of one-half hour was allocated for each interview. The study consultant followed the participant or Guide interview guidelines (Appendixes D and E) and transcribed the content of each on paper. Interview content was subsequently word-processed for qualitative analysis and storage.

The interview process was planned to provide participants and Guides with the opportunity to comment reflectively with assured confidentiality to a consistent set of topics. Items were selected based on content of HOPE materials and an assessment of topics that would most likely contribute to the study hypotheses. Thus people were invited to share if and how their experiences with HOPE had contributed to the life experience, and the qualities that each person determined necessary to be an effective Guide. The content of each interview was transcribed to paper and subsequently word-processed for analysis and storage.

Data Analysis

Quantitative data was gathered by survey of present and past HOPE participants and Guides. Demographic data were analyzed using descriptive methods to determine distribution of gender, age, educational level, residence by county, and frequency of group participation.

A second survey, the HOPE Group Questionnaire, gathered the subjects' level of agreement with fifteen HOPE-related statements. Level of agreement was analyzed according to range, mean, and standard deviation. Use of this method, measuring participants' perceptions about HOPE, acknowledges that this study's phenomenon of interest is the lived experience of those who participate in HOPE.

Qualitative analysis followed phenomenological guidelines to analyze group observations, interviews, and the focus group content. It is the lived experience of each person within HOPE that is the interest of this study. Each HOPEr is the one who provides the most accurate information about his/her life, its meaning, and if or how HOPE has affected that life. "The body, the world, and the concerns, unique to each person, are the context within which that person can be understood" (Burns & Grove, 2001, p. 65).

Group observation and interview content guidelines were drawn from HOPE's philosophy and approved by H.O.P.E.'s Board of Directors as part of the study design. (See Appendixes C and D). The study consultant transcribed group meetings and interviews by hand after which the content of each encounter was word processed in entirety.

The following methods were used to analyze group observations and individual interviews:

- Theme and content were guided by the observation and interview guidelines,
- Observations and interviews were transcribed and reread a minimum of five times: first, at the time of word processing; second, at the time of coding (see next item); third, at the time of compiling comments by group or interview category; fourth, as review of additional themes of interest emerged through the coding process; and fifth, to validate or adjust the category outcomes.
- Words, phrases, and sentences were coded following the themes of the observation and interview guidelines, along with categories of interest that emerged through clarifying iterations. Themes were drawn from the HOPE philosophy.
- Participant and Guide content areas were coded and categorized separately. Outcomes were analyzed comparatively, such as in the review of the Guide traits, to enrich depth of discussion regarding HOPE's application and outcomes.
- Narrative discussion of categories and thematic meanings were complemented by numerical analysis. This method was used to distinguish areas of greater or lesser agreement with HOPE principles.
- The HOPE Story was sent to the H.O.P.E. Board of Directors and a sample of study participants for review and comment.

Results

Quantitative Findings

Data presented in this section include demographic information, group participation summaries of the South Paris and Portland Group meetings, and results of the level of agreement questionnaire. Participants represented in the following discussion of data were part of a purposive sample of present and past HOPE group participants and Guides who were recruited for the study by the primary investigator. The total sample size of this study is 50, including Hamilton who was interviewed as HOPE's senior Guide.

Demographic Information

Study packets were distributed to 50 group participants and Guides. . Twenty-three people returned the demographic questionnaire, representing 46% of the sample. The balance of participants agreed to participate in the study and chose to limit their involvement to participation during group observations.

Both men and women participated in this study. Table 1 depicts gender distribution based on demographic questionnaire responses, with seven men representing just over 30% of the sample and sixteen women representing almost 70% of the sample. Interestingly, these figures closely parallel the distribution data of the Portland group as discussed in the *Group Participation Summary* section. These figures are of note despite a modest return of demographic questionnaires.

Table 1 Gender

		Frequency	Percent	Valid Percent	Cumulative Percent
Valid	Female	16	69.6	69.6	69.6
	Male	7	30.4	30.4	100.0
	Total	23	100.0	100.0	

Table 2 represents age distribution of those who returned the demographic questionnaire. Ten-year interval age measures beginning at 20 years and extending to 60-plus years were used to collect age information. Although over 95% of this sample falls in the 40 year to 60-plus year age range, it is interesting to note the presence of someone who is in her/his twenties. These measures include people who are now in their fifties or sixties and who have been attending HOPE for a decade or more. The average age of this sample falls between 50 and 59 years.

Table 2 Age

		Frequency	Percent	Valid Percent	Cumulative Percent
Valid	20-29	1	4.3	4.3	4.3
	40-49	8	34.8	34.8	39.1
	50-59	5	21.7	21.7	60.9
	60 +	9	39.1	39.1	100.0
	Total	23	100.0	100.0	

Table 3 shows that the 23 people represented in this sample all report some level of college education with almost 35% (n=8) having education at least at the Master's level.

Table 3 Education

		Frequency	Percent	Valid Percent	Cumulative Percent
Valid	Bachelor's degree	6	26.1	26.1	26.1
	Master's degree +	8	34.8	34.8	60.9
	Some college	9	39.1	39.1	100.0
	Total	23	100.0	100.0	

Table 4 details the county of residence. Ten participants and Guides (45.5%) who completed the demographic questionnaire live in Cumberland County, the site of the Portland Group and four (18.2%) live in Oxford County, the site of the South Paris Group. Two of the people represented in this sample (9.1%) and who participated in Guide trainings, live out of state. The remaining people are distributed evenly across county of residence, with one each (4.5%) living in Androscoggin, Franklin, Sagadahoc, York, Waldo, and Kennebec, and one county of residence unreported.

Table 4 County of Residence

		Frequency	Percent	Valid Percent	Cumulative Percent
Valid	Androscoggin	1	4.3	4.5	4.5
	Cumberland	10	43.5	45.5	50.0
	Franklin	1	4.3	4.5	54.5
	Oxford	4	17.4	18.2	72.7
	Sagadahoc	1	4.3	4.5	77.3
	York	1	4.3	4.5	81.8
	Waldo	1	4.3	4.5	86.4
	out of state	2	8.7	9.1	95.5
	Kennebec	1	4.3	4.5	100.0
	Total	22	95.7	100.0	
Missing	System	1	4.3		
Total		23	100.0		

Group Participation Summary

HOPE Group participation figures represent those of both present and past group participants and Guides. Table 5 displays the number of years people have participated in a HOPE Group by range. It is of particular interest to note that almost 41% of this sample attended meetings for up to two years.

Table 5 Number of Years Participated

		Frequency	Percent	Valid Percent	Cumulative Percent
Valid	<1 year	6	26.1	27.3	27.3
	1-2 years	3	13.0	13.6	40.9
	2-3 years	1	4.3	4.5	45.5
	3-5 years	5	21.7	22.7	68.2
	6+ years	7	30.4	31.8	100.0
	Total	22	95.7	100.0	
Missing	System	1	4.3		
Total		23	100.0		

Thirty-five people were present in the groups that were observed. Of these, 17 (48.6%) agreed to participate in interviews. Distribution of numbers participating in interviews by group were: Five from South Paris, representing 40% of the observed group; eleven from Portland, representing 55% of those observed; and, one from Hallowell, representing 33% of those observed. Another two group participants, one each from Portland and Hallowell, who report current ongoing attendance, participated in the interview process although neither was present at the time of a group observation.

HOPE participants and Guides were asked during the telephone interviews (n=31) to share how they learned about HOPE Groups and to state their reason for choosing to attend. Content from the interviews revealed that thirteen (42%) learned about HOPE from a professional source such as a physician or counselor, eight (26%) were encouraged to go to a HOPE meeting by a family member or a friend, six (19%) learned about HOPE from a community source such as a newspaper or gathering place, and four (13%) first heard about HOPE during an educational event or support group meeting.

Reasons for attending HOPE meetings were clustered according to diagnosis if that was revealed during the interview.

Twelve people (39%) were attracted to HOPE for support with psychological health, ten (32%) because of a cancer diagnosis, two (6.5%) for support following the death of a spouse, one (3%) because of cardiac disease, and six (19%) for other reasons or those not revealed. Five of the thirty-one people interviewed (16%) have attended HOPE Groups because of a family member's health challenges. Their reasons for being part of HOPE are included in these figures.

It is important to note that while group participants were informed about the study and invited to take part in an interview, the consultant provided minimal encouragement to do so. This approach is in keeping with study protocol and, more importantly, HOPE's philosophy regarding choice, mutual consideration, and respect (Hamilton, 1993).

South Paris

A total of twelve people attended South Paris meetings during the observation period. Six of these people attended meetings two to six times. Average meeting attendance numbered just over five. One member of this group who attended two meetings requested that her words not be transcribed. Her wishes were honored according to study protocol. Five of the twelve participants, representing just over 40% of this group, agreed to participate in interviews. Of these, one was conducted in person and the others were completed by telephone.

Table 6 depicts the dates, group composition, and participant to Guide ratio of conversational comment. Counting the total number of participant comments and dividing this figure by the total number of Guide comments attained this ratio. This ratio is of importance when one considers that HOPE group process is a mutual experience. The Guide is a participant who is present to be part of the group dialogue and to assure that the meeting follows the principles and guidelines set forth in *The Gold Book* (Hamilton, 1993).

Table 6 The South Paris Group

Date	5/18	5/25	6/1	6/15	6/22	6/29
Composition	5 ♀	8 ♀	5 ♀	4 ♀	6 ♀	3: 2 ♀, 1 ♂
Ken is present	No	Yes	Yes	Yes	Yes	Yes
Participant: Guide ratio of comment	N/A	2.36:1	3.58:1	1.68:1	3.05:1	1.59:1

Portland

A total of 20 people attended the Portland meetings during the observation period, as presented in Table 7. Fifteen of these people attended the meetings two or more times during the six-week period with 50% of the total attending at least three meetings. Average meeting attendance numbered just over twelve. This level of attendance is worthy of contemplation since these meetings occurred during the height of Maine's vacation season.

Table 7 The Portland Group

Date	7/11	7/18	7/25	8/1	8/8	8/15
Composition	14: 7♀, 7♂	15: 10♀, 5♂	12: 7♀, 5♂	12: 7♀, 5♂	10: 7♀, 3♂	11: 8♀, 3♂
Percent of this group who are men	50%	33%	42%	42%	30%	27%
Ken is present	Yes	Yes	Yes	Yes	No	Yes
Participant: Guide ratio of comment	5.65:1	3.5:1	3.95:1	8.33:1	N/A	4.14:1

HOPE Group Questionnaire: Level of Agreement

Twenty people, seventeen of whom are present HOPE participants, comprise the portion of the sample that completed both the HOPE Group Questionnaire and the demographic questionnaire. Three respondents were past participants, including one person who went on to become a long term Guide. The HOPE Group Questionnaire is displayed in Appendix B. As previously described, subjects were asked to respond by level of agreement to 15 statements derived from HOPE materials, such as *The Gold Book* (Hamilton, 1993).

Table 8 displays the mean analysis of the responses by statement. The statements with the highest level of agreement are statements one, four, and twelve. These statements show the smallest standard deviation. Statements five, nine, and fourteen are the statements that were selected to have an inverse relationship to limit bias. These statements do in fact show the lowest mean, with two, numbers nine and fourteen, having the largest standard deviations.

Table 8 Level of Agreement with HOPE statements: Mean Analysis and Standard Deviation

(STAT means Statement: See Appendix B)

	N	Minimum	Maximum	Mean	Std. Dev.
STAT1	20	3	4	3.85	.366
STAT2	20	3	4	3.75	.444
STAT3	20	3	4	3.65	.489
STAT4	20	3	4	3.80	.410
STAT5	20	1	3	1.85	.745
STAT6	20	3	4	3.60	.503
STAT7	20	3	4	3.65	.489
STAT8	19	1	4	3.21	.855
STAT9	20	1	4	2.70	1.031
STAT10	19	1	4	3.16	.765
STAT11	20	3	4	3.65	.489
STAT12	20	3	4	3.90	.308
STAT13	20	3	4	3.75	.444
STAT14	20	1	4	2.80	1.105
STAT15	20	3	4	3.65	.489
Valid N (listwise)	18				

Demographic data and level of agreement with statements were subjected to Pearson two-tailed correlations in which a $p=0.01$ is considered significant. Table 9 is the correlations matrix that depicts the relationships that were revealed. Demographic correlations suggest that age and years of participation are positively related with the number of group meetings one has attended. Correlations were primarily positive with one yielding a negative linear relationship. That one is the correlation between years of group participation and statement thirteen that is a Guide-related statement. The suggestion is that higher years of participation do not positively correlate with this statement. Apparently participants experience mutual care and consideration despite a limited length of participation in a HOPE group.

Of particular note are the strong correlations between statements two and three, and eight and ten as these reveal consistency of attitude within-person. Items six and thirteen link one's belief about HOPE participation with one's observation about the Guide's contribution to mutual care and respect. Items thirteen and fifteen show a strong correlation that suggests how the power of loving focus on each person contributes to the perception that time together is considerate.

Table 9 Demographic Data and Agreement with Statements Correlation Matrix

	Age	Years Part	#3	#9	#10	#12	#13	#15
Years Part							r= -.638 p=.002	
Group Part	r=.581 p=.009	r=.647 p=.003						
#2			r=.787 p=.000				r=.577 p=.008	
#5				r=.623 p=.003				
#6							r=.707 p=.000	
#8					r=.881 p=.000			
#12							r=.577 p=.008	
#13								r=.787 p=.000

Qualitative Findings

Data presented in this section include findings from group observations, interviews, and the Guide focus group, with references to the Appendixes. Data were collected as described previously in the data collection section.

Group Dialogue Content

Table 10 demonstrates the consistency of overall content between groups. Statements included in this content analysis reflect topics initiated primarily by participants rather than the Guide. Not all statements that were part of a group transcription were assigned a content area. Those statements that were not selected were outside of the conversational rhythm and flow or were its extensions.

Analysis of statements was selected by following the tenets of attitudinal healing as presented in *The Gold Book* (Hamilton, 1993). Guideline one agrees to "help the group focus on attitudinal healing by letting go of fear and conflict, and seeing life in a peaceful and loving way" (p. 4). This conveys affirmation of life and its process by embracing life's wholeness. This led to identifying conversational content that affirmed life because of the peace and love evoked by a person's words.

The letting go that is invited through the first HOPE Group Guideline supports the individual to "learn to live in each moment" (Hamilton, 1993, p.2). This fifth statement of the HOPE Group Opening embraces the ability to step into a place of neutrality and acceptance. The statements associated with this way of being emerged with a tone of observation. These are called neutral content.

When one is caught in the quagmire that life can present, a sense of limitation and feeling torn asunder can become the current reality. Life and the ability to find peace of mind become fragmented by the hold of guilt, fear, and conflict (Hamilton, 1993). A person caught in this place conveys their loss of inner peace through use of language that connotes limited choice, disrupted power, and a judgmental sense of self. These statements are referred to as life-limiting content.

Life affirming content includes those statements that reflect the whole of life, promote inner peace, value each person's process, and do not view death fearfully (Hamilton, 1993). Examples of life affirming statements that emerged during meetings of each group include:

- I've learned to take care of myself.
- This is the place I come to because I am accepted.
- Just wonderful you are doing what you are doing.
- The messages come through when it's quiet.
- It's about the quality of life.
- Without life, there's no way to experience miracles and I think they're fine.
- I have a desire to help myself and others.
- I think the most powerful thing is example... and compassion. I am much more compassionate.

Statements that convey neutral content are those that convey a sense of acceptance. This state of acceptance emerges from living in the moment and the ability to "let go of the past and of the future" (Hamilton, 1993, p. 2). Examples of statements made from a place of observation include:

- I'm an optimist rooted in reality.
- I'm staying out of it.
- It's taken me years to get the head and the heart together.
- It's new for me because I used to plan around other people.
- I am more aware and honest.
- The decision I make when I'm angry is different than when I'm peaceful.
- It'd be great if someone drifted into my life but it's not going to heal me.
- Joy was something that only happened once in a while.

Life limiting statements are those rooted in powerlessness, fear, guilt, and a feeling of fragmentation (Hamilton, 1993, p.3). Examples of life limiting statements include:

- There's no excuse.
- Hard to be able to do anything and the helplessness of not being able to make it better.
- Trouble... I can get in trouble standing still.
- Don't have an answer... it pisses me off.
- And I'm back in the same state, oh, anyway....
- If I'd only listened to myself years ago.
- Acceptance doesn't work for me.
- I want my life back.

Table 10 depicts the comparative analysis within and between the South Paris and Portland groups related to the three levels of content. There is a close margin of consistency between the two groups when considering life affirming, neutral, and life limiting comment. Additionally, consistency is close, within four percentage points, across content areas when compared by ratios.

Table 10 Comparisons of Meeting Participants' Statements

	Life Affirming Content	Neutral Content	Life Limiting Content
South Paris: N=146 statements	N=56 statements 38% of total	N=47 statements 32% of total	N=43 statements 29% of total
Portland N=366 statements	N=148 statements 40% of total	N=115 statements 31% of total	N=103 statements 28% of total
Comparative ratios of South Paris and Portland statements by content area	South Paris= 37.8% of Portland (56/148)	South Paris=40.9% of Portland (47/115)	South Paris=41.7% of Portland (43/103)

Topical Content

HOPE Groups agree to "recognize the importance of each person's process, and in this way we create a safe atmosphere for the whole group" (Hamilton, 1993, p. 4). This third HOPE Group Guideline aligns with the sixth in which "we agree to risk and expose our own emotional states, and thus we share our common experience" (p. 4). The common experience is life, for people within a HOPE Group may or may not walk through the door with a specific malady.

Early in the group observation process it became apparent that people in HOPE groups talk about a wide range of topics. Some are mundane, common topics that seem typical to the daily life of every person. Others are lofty, esoteric, and not what might be considered part of mainstream thought or conversation. The topics emerged as each person stepped into the safety of group conversation. In this setting, each person was able to authentically reveal her/himself, share innermost emotions, and flow with individual process.

Topics selected for analysis were those brought into conversation by a participant. The analysis process involved three steps. Topics were listed that were part of each meeting's dialogue. Second, topics that arose in more than one meeting were counted for repeat occurrences across meetings and tallied. Lastly, topics that were part of the dialogue of four or more meetings were selected for analysis. Each group had six topics that emerged with that level of frequency.

Table 11 depicts the conversational topics that emerged with greatest frequency during the six-week observation periods in the South Paris and Portland Groups.

Table 11   Topical Content of HOPE Group Meetings

Topic	South Paris Topic Frequency	Portland Topic Frequency
Health issues	6	3
Their children: young or adult	6	4
Divorce/former spouse/partner	6	1
Parents (of group members)	2	6
Work/jobs	5	3
Physicians/medical care	5	3
Houses	4	2
Love	1	4
Depression	2	4
Peace		4
Death	3	4
Another HOPE member	1	4

Participant Interview Content

Participant interviews were conducted following the guidelines found in Appendix D. Each interview was recorded on paper and transcribed, after which all interviews were reviewed for content. Content followed the interview guidelines to gather reasons for HOPE participation, influence on one's life, personal meaning derived from the HOPE Group experience, comparison with other support group experiences, and the Guide qualities one valued. As content was clustered within each of the areas mentioned, it became apparent that HOPE offered people a breadth and depth of meaning and life experience that expanded on the outlined content areas. These topic areas, in addition to those originally outlined for the interview process, are presented in Table 12 to prepare the reader for discussion of this content with that of

HOPE Groups and their experienced, observed, and perceived value. Table 12 displays the number of statements included in each cluster and the percent of statements related to the number of interviews. Table 13 displays examples of statements from the four highest ranked clusters.

Table 12   Interview Content Analysis

Statement cluster (Participant Interviews: N=25)	Number of statements	Statement % of interviews
Are clear about what drew them to the HOPE Group.	N=22	88%
Identify that they were already on a path of personal exploration and development when they first attended a HOPE meeting.	N=7	28%
View HOPE as a community in which they can reveal their authentic selves.	N=13	52%
Experience HOPE as a place of giving and receiving.	N=17	68%
Express the ways in which HOPE has influenced their lives.	N=25	100%
HOPE guides people in the process of reframing attitudes by creating an environment of healing (process-focused).	N=27 Note: Two comments made by two participants	108%
HOPE fosters an environment that cultivates the dance between group process and personal reflection.	N=14	56%
HOPE invites each person to explore life and its potentials/possibilities as the container for resolving problems and experiencing healing (life-focused).	N=15	60%
HOPE's distinctions as a support group include:	N=21	84%
I value HOPE because:	N=20	80%
HOPE is a place for learning what works for others.	N=13	52%

Table 13   Sample Participant Interview Statements

Statement Cluster	Examples
Are clear about what drew them to the HOPE Group.	* Lots of reasons. A safe environment to discuss... I'm smart enough to know that I don't know it all. * I did it for personal growth and for my husband to survive.
Express the ways in which HOPE has influenced their lives.	* How I've approached my life has just been a little more present to each moment. There's been a reinvention of the relationship with my life and my family. * Honestly believe I wouldn't be here without Ken and HOPE.
HOPE guides people in the process of reframing attitudes by creating an environment of healing.	* I experience more joy. It is encouraging and I am making changes and am still on a spiritual journey. I am encouraged by HOPE. * I came alive into my own self.
HOPE's distinctions as a support group include:	* HOPE focuses on the whole person. Identifies the whole as therapeutic. * HOPE is about optimism and solving problems and joy. It is about living with and learning from the pain.

Guide Interview Content

Six Guides in addition to Hamilton participated in interviews. Four of these live in Maine and were HOPE Group participants prior to moving into the Guide role. One person continues her participation in a HOPE Group, aside from her past experience as a Guide. Three Guides living in Maine led HOPE Groups for durations of two to eight years; one has been guiding HOPE Groups for over five years and continues to do so. Two Guides who live in other states have a wealth of other group experience with limited experience leading a HOPE Group. Five of the Guides are female and one is a male. Four of the six participated in the Focus Group that is summarized later in this section.

Three of the six Guides learned about HOPE through a friend or relative, with the remaining three learning about HOPE from Bernie Siegel, the Rowe Center in Massachusetts, and the Center for Attitudinal Healing in California. Guides were asked the reason for fulfilling this role within HOPE. Responses range from "it was a vehicle to express a desire to create a center of healing that had a spiritual focus" to "I like to give back... we had benefited so much from the meetings we attended." Other comments included "I tuned into negative feelings to forgive," "I liked the attitude and the work," and "what I loved was it wasn't redundant or about keeping score and telling you how to live your life."

When asked how HOPE had influenced their lives, Guides reported a growth in trust and compassion; knowing one has choices and meaning derived from attitudinal healing; an awareness that HOPE was part of one's life path; heightened confidence and the focus for reflection; a shift in thinking that happens with HOPE's influence; and, the ability to rely on inner strength. All of the Guides interviewed have knowledge of or experience with support groups other than HOPE. They offered their perspective about HOPE's distinctions. "HOPE is about life beyond the challenge." "It works to have the group do the work, not having it be the leader. It's about holding each other accountable." "We all have stories. Something positive has to come out of the encounter." "It's mostly safe, there are no shoulds. It grows with you. You don't outgrow it. It is different every time and someone comes in with wisdom. It is something else to take home and it hasn't failed me yet." "HOPE gives opportunity to tune into your power within you and get it inside, not outside."

The Guide qualities reported by Guides are summarized with those reflected upon by participants in the closing portion of the results presentation.

Guide Focus Group Content

Present and past HOPE Guides were invited to participate in a focus group that was part of a daylong celebration of H.O.P.E. at the Ripley Center in South Paris. The focus group purpose was for people to dialogue about their individual and collective experiences with guiding HOPE groups. Eight people, including Ken Hamilton, participated in this group. Six of the eight have participated in HOPE Guide training. It is their conversational content that is included in this summary. The Guides stated that they chose to engage in the focus group to "gain light and wisdom with the process," "to reinforce the principles [that are used] in my everyday life," and to learn "to stay successful and confident" in the Guide's role.

Analysis of content transcribed from this meeting revealed three threads of dialogue. These are who the guide is and what s/he brings to the role, the HOPE meeting process, and what is emerging within the HOPE experience. This third content area spanned from a need for more clarity about HOPE and its direction, to an exploration of "what Ken does to help people to move forward."

The Guide was identified as someone who can "let go of attachments to how a person is supposed to live their life" and, with consistency, creates an atmosphere that feels safe to participants and the Guide alike. The Guide comes "from our consciousness of wholeness," "leaves ego at the door," and is "a person of compassion." The Guides reflected that an "average person... who has a calling [can be] a facilitator."

That person may have a high school education or be from the healing arts. People share the call to serve and derive the basic information to form and guide a group from the HOPE Guide's training. Focus group members stated that the value of Guide training is increased confidence and the realization that "we are guides unto ourselves and have our own style." A central experience for Guides is to "take the [HOPE] principles and work them from your own core." This leads to an awareness to "trust the process" and the practice of "always doing their own healing."

Dialogue that emerged about the HOPE meeting process centered on *The Gold Book* (Hamilton, 1993) and how its power invites the group "to be responsible for itself." This conversation became an exploration of group dynamics and difficulties, and how to use HOPE's principles to reframe negativity and disruption when it arises. "It is about how we treat each other... this is the agreement and to remind people of that." When the group feels that it is becoming fragmented, either within a meeting or from meeting to meeting, *The Gold Book* serves as the contract that invites opening to wholeness. The Guide's ability to be present contributes to an atmosphere of openness. Therein the Guide gently casts light on each person and invites the answer to the question "what are you here for?" The question can be as much about one's presence in the HOPE group as it is about seeking life meaning. The Guide knows this and supports individuals and the group to reframe words and attitudes that lead to fragmentation. This experience of guiding the group in its evolution to wholeness is one of mutual participation that includes group participants and the HOPE principles and guidelines as described in *The Gold Book*.

HOPE's process invites the emergence of new ways of being for the individual, the group, and the organization. The Guides' focus group dialogue touched on each of these, with one aspect contributing to the potential of another. The desire of a Guide "to gain light and wisdom with this process" resonates with the intention set when "one pulls in the fragments to answer the question." This intention sets the tone for healing, yet acknowledges that people will come to that consciousness in varied ways and at different times. The focus group Guides were passionate about how to further inform their role within HOPE. One seeks "guidance [to become a Guide]; even though I'm in the healing arts, I don't have the confidence. In my profession as a speech pathologist, they tell us to counsel but not how. How can I learn to do that?" Another states, "I have the confidence and am a good facilitator. I want to explore what Ken does to help people to move forward and to move HOPE and HOPErs forward." These comments speak from a very personal place about the compelling nature of HOPE, and of each Guide's calling to contribute to HOPE's potential.

Guide Qualities as Reported by Interviewees

The interviews conducted with participants and Guides requested that people share their opinions about HOPE Guide qualities. Their words and phrases were transcribed and synthesized to observe pattern emergence. Some qualities, such as being non-judgmental and possessing wisdom, emerged as repeated themes. Other traits or qualities were noted once or aligned with comment offered by another person. The pattern that emerged revealed three categories of Guide qualities that had meaning for HOPE participants and Guides. These are communication skills, self-awareness, and relationship-centered awareness. The term relationship-centered awareness used here recognizes that the HOPE Guide is conscious of the numerous relationships that influence what emerges, or is kept silent, within each meeting's experience. The relationships include each person's relationship with him or herself, their internal and external environments, and their story heretofore and as it is unfolding, to name a few. Appendix F displays the content drawn from the interviews.

The Guide qualities described by participants were categorized separately from those of the Guides. Qualities identified by all interviewees were compared with those described by Hamilton in The HOPE Guide's Manual (1996). What emerged were horizontal threads that weave from one group's perspective to the next, and are supported by Hamilton's description of the qualities necessary to be a HOPE Guide. These threads, personal traits, level of function, and qualities of transcendence, are demonstrated through the Guide's self-awareness and relationship-centered awareness.

Interviewee Suggestions

The Interview Guidelines associated with this study did not include gathering suggestions from either participants or Guides. A set of suggestions occurred naturally as part of the interview process. Content of twenty-two of the thirty-one interviews conducted revealed that participants and Guides had suggestions to offer for HOPE's benefit. These clustered into the content areas of meeting conduct (n=8), disruptive behaviors (n=4), HOPE readiness (n=3), personal tools (n=3), other (n=3), clinical services (n=2), and mentoring (n=2). A few interviewees made comments that fell into more than one area. Seventeen of the comments address content that is or may become part of the Guide training.

Meeting conduct content was addressed with the greatest frequency. Participants felt that the meeting was different when Ken was not present, although they stated that the group is responsible for guiding itself. "There is the ground rules piece. It is important for any meeting and for each person to know that." Participants have particular views on how and what is appropriate for a HOPE meeting. Suggestions included limiting length of a person's comments, using Guided Imagery, judicious use of stories and quantum theory discussion, and identifying when someone's needs "go beyond what HOPE can do."

Participants' concerns about people who exhibit behaviors that are disruptive to the group interfaces with meeting conduct. "I don't think she was trying to wreck the group. When she was there, the numbers had dropped and now they have come back up." Another participant shared a feeling of diminished safety within the group because of another person. "It changed the whole atmosphere... there is responsibility to the group." Two other participants questioned if it is within HOPE's scope to address personal safety beyond the group. "There is an opportunity to form friendships. This can be a support and a red flag. In these groups there is need to use care... with people who [may be] emotionally challenged."

The Guides suggested methods to address the areas of importance noted by participants. One suggestion is to assure that the principles are "expanded upon in the training. They are there by implication but may need to do [these] as a line by line in conversation." Another Guide follows this thinking by addressing the importance of experiential training and mentoring. "I know I need more to be a Guide. There was so much presented and no time to discuss, to practice, and to process... need more experiential... more on *The Gold Book* and its importance... The importance of mentoring." Another Guide stated the importance of experiential learning, such as mentoring with a Guide, to add to the class and its materials.

A Guide who wants to learn more about how to guide people with moving forward offered this reflective comment. "There's something else... to teach to keep it in motion: the right question to bring them there [to the place of answering one's own question]." It was implied that this communication form might positively affect the group's dynamic when a person with disruptive behaviors is present. "A group can be ruined by too much stuff; those who are power hungry."

Discussion

HOPE Group demographic information comparisons made with those in the literature and the general population reveal both commonalities and differences that contribute to findings, conclusions, and planning for HOPE's future. Gender distribution represented in this study compares quite favorably with other support group study populations. HOPE participants who submitted demographic information are 69.6% female and 30.4% male. Gender distribution for those participating in cancer support groups was 83.9% female and 16.1% male in a sample of 62 people (Grande, Myers, & Sutton, 2005). A study sample of 72 women and men who lived with chronic pain or psychosocial difficulties (Arthur & Edwards, 2005), showed a distribution of 78% female and 22%

male. Data from these studies are contrasted with gender distribution of people in a support group for those with HIV, wherein males represented 65.7% (n=23) of a sample of 35 people, and 31.4% (n=11) were female, with 2.9% (n=1) missing (Walsh, Roetzer, & Minnett, 2006).

The average age of the HOPE sample (n=23) falls between 50 and 59 years. Arthur and Edwards (2005), in their evaluation of people with chronic pain and complex psychosocial difficulties, noted that the mean age of 72 participants was 56.39 years. Maine women with breast cancer had an age range of 42-76 years (Zeigler, Smith, & Fawcett, 2004).

HOPE participants have a high level of education when compared with support group findings and Maine's general population. One hundred percent of this sample (n=23) reported having 'some college,' with 26% having a Bachelor's degree, and almost 35% being prepared at the Master's level or higher. This level of education is an increase in that reported by HOPE participants in 1991. The study of Maine women living with breast cancer (Zeigler, Smith, & Fawcett, 2004) revealed that the ten participants had high school to graduate school education, although distribution data was not published. Support group participation by 35 people with HIV revealed that 11.4% had less than 12 years of education. Recent census data (U. S. Census Bureau, 2000) related to educational levels, reveals that in Maine 85.4% of adults 25 years and older are high school graduates and 22.9% of the same age group have a bachelor's degree or higher.

The results of the HOPE Group level of agreement questionnaire resulted in several pertinent observations. The first is that the statement with the highest mean score and lowest standard deviation was one related to the Guide's conduct. This response level affirms that the Guide's recognition of the importance of each person's process creates a safe atmosphere for the whole group. This factor is significantly correlated with each participant's belief that the power of choice rests within. The finding of creating a caring community is one of the unique features of self-help groups that is described in the literature (Leung & Arthur, 2004). Two other participant belief and Guide conduct statements demonstrated significant correlation, suggesting that moving from fear and anger to happiness and joy is influenced by time spent in mutual care, consideration, and respect.

Positive correlations were found between participant age and the length of participation with the number of groups attended. This finding was not surprising whereas the statistically significant inverse relationship between length of group participation with Guide conduct that promotes mutual care, consideration, and respect, was revealing. Therefore people who have been in the group for less than one year feel the same level of benefit of time together as those who have a longer history with the group. This outcome is reflective of the role of the healthcare professional in groups as one that "contributes to ensuring equal worth and meaningful togetherness within the group" (Adamsen & Rasmussen, 2003, p. 32).

One test of the consistency of HOPE's framework and practical application is evident when one examines the content between the two groups that were the focus of this study. The groups demonstrated consistency within two percentage points of each other regarding life affirming, neutral, and life limiting comments. Additionally, when content areas from the two groups were clustered into topic areas, there was a high degree of consistency in these too. Of the twelve topic areas that were frequently repeated in either one or both groups, five were discussed three or more times in both groups. These topics were the participants' children, either young or adult, health issues, work, physicians and health care, and death. Two observations arise because of this. The first is that while there is some consistency in HOPE dialogue, there is wide variation that is reflective of the people involved. The second is that the topics that were repeated are balanced between the concerns of day-to-day life and one's health.

These observations are one of the means of describing the ways in which HOPE is focused on life and wholeness. Within the context of HOPE, death is discussed as an existential phenomenon, a transformative experience that is a natural part of life's cycle, and one that is shared by all.

Interviews and focus groups serve as two means for gathering qualitative information for comparative purposes and from which to gain new insights (Dadich, 2006; Paquet et al., 2005). HOPE participants reported through interviews the nature of the group's environment and how it contributes to shifts in attitude toward healing. Leung and Arthur (2004) found that one benefit of groups was how "they increase members' coping skills through the provision of information and sharing of experiences and problem solutions" (p. 238).

This holistic form of support has been identified as the sort where people can share information and seek solutions without the "over-protectiveness of family members" (Paquet et al., 2005, p. 574). A participatory approach is described as one that offers people mutuality through which quality of life is improved and anxiety is reduced. HOPE participants and Guides who were interviewed and contributed to the focus group identified the meetings as a place to learn what worked for others. They reflected on the meaning of learning about authors and books from the Guide and others within the group. The use of books and audiovisuals is described as one through which a person can develop a "life long therapeutic relationship" (Lampropoulos & Spengler, 2005, p. 51). Both HOPE Guides and participants continually referred to *The Gold Book*. They describe its use in personal life for reflection as well as during the meeting. Thus use of this resource becomes a tangible expression of HOPE that bridges the time between meetings and becomes a relational reminder of HOPE's meaning and promise.

One of the challenges for HOPE in the future, particularly as it moves more into clinical settings, is describing its unique form as a group. This factor is significant when one considers that self-help groups, for instance, have been identified as a viable treatment option for the future (Norcross, Hedges, & Prochaska, 2002). Another outcome of this Delphi study about the future of psychotherapy indicated several other therapeutic options that are part of HOPE's process as being those predicted to increase by 2010. Options include problem-solving techniques, self-change techniques, and interpersonal support (p. 320). Self-help groups are defined as being supportive, educational, led from within the group, an option to address a life-disrupting event, and offer personal growth as the group's primary purpose (Leung & Arthur, 2004, p. 233). HOPE enfolds some of these attributes yet is overall broader. Adamsen and Rasmussen's (2003) discussion of self-help groups for people with cancer adopts a broad view of the group's purpose. Their interpretation is that the group "focuses on social processes and collectively creates new possibilities" that "creates a basis for patients to come to grips with their change process" (p. 33).

This description of self-help aligns with HOPE although it does not address the intrinsic value that is consistently described by HOPE participants and Guides. This consistency flowed throughout this 2006 study and does so even when one retrospectively considers the studies conducted in 1991, 1997, and 1998. "The conversation isn't so much directed toward the physical ailment that is bothering the person but how the whole process is shaping his/her attitudes" (Brophy, Skillings, & Chandler, 1991, p. 5). A 2006 interview participant describes HOPE value as "the personal growth and what I have learned... I look at the hammer marks that are the coin I am."

This strength of consistency supports a view that HOPE's framework is grounded on a solid foundation. Use of *The Gold Book* as a collective and individual reference tool highlights it as a bridge between theory and application. This resource's value and use, in the words of one Guide, is considered "non-negotiable." Other interventions however may be optional tools for a Guide to consider using based on group needs. These include use of the breath, guided imagery, meditation, and visualization, to name a few. A number of self-care methods align with HOPE's philosophy because each supports wholeness and focuses on life process. Some participants who were interviewed suggested that inclusion of the aforementioned methods is a necessity for HOPE. Each method has value but does not define what HOPE is. The guidelines and how these are applied are the living description of HOPE. Self-care methods, like books, which are brought to the dialogue by a participant or the Guide, serve as optional resources and interventions.

One area that uniquely defines HOPE is that of the Guide, both by description and participation. People who contributed to the interview process stated that the person who fulfills this role must be someone who displays wisdom and maturity, is non-judgmental and a good listener, and possesses a level of self-awareness that invites the ego to step aside in order to be compassionately centered with another as s/he seeks solutions for life's conflicts and suffering. Adamsen and Rasmussen (2003) refer to this role as that of "social networker" (p. 34). Their study of nurses who facilitated support groups for people with cancer identifies a set of dimensions that demonstrate the professional role in these groups. The dimensions with the aligned function or way of being include: focus and "togetherness around life situation as a resource"; interaction and participant, and interactive group process; responsibility and "the control of the situation is shared among patients/the nurse"; knowledge and "the knowledge belongs to the participant and is based on subjective personal experience"; and, vision and "universalizing, generalizing, de-individualizing, anti-stigmatizing" (p. 34). These dimensions describe HOPE as it is presented in *The Gold Book* and as both participants and Guides have conveyed their experiences.

The suggestions offered during the interviews are worthy of consideration, particularly those that touch on the preparation and support of Guides. Mentoring of Guides provides supervision and support as they adjust to their role and participation in a HOPE group. This guidance provides for dialogue about topics such as group dynamics, participatory action, and distinguishing between one's professional role and that of HOPE Guide.

Conclusions

Implications for Practice

The findings of this study suggest that HOPE offers people a consistent framework from which to explore new ways of being and participating in life. HOPE's focus on wholeness, peace, and letting go of fear offers solace for those who seek life meaning and renewal of Self. The results of this study, and those from the last fifteen years, suggest that HOPE's framework and its philosophy, psychology, and concepts have stood the test of time.

It is timely for HOPE to be integrated within clinical settings, even as it expands within community settings. When these are woven together it optimizes the opportunity for seamless care. Group care is one method that is identified as potentially fulfilling a need for quality, compassionate care that is cost efficient (Leung & Arthur, 2004; Zabalegui et al., 2005).

This study's findings point to the importance of the Guide's role in representing and conveying the essence of HOPE. The Guide selection, preparation, and support functions are essential to the provision of compassionate care that is consistent with HOPE's principles, guidelines, and practices. These functions assure care and service for HOPE groups in both clinical and community settings. Guide qualities as described in this study and *The HOPE Guide's Manual* (Hamilton, 1996), are core components regardless of the discipline that the Guide practices. Thus the person and his/her personal traits are primary to the Guide's role and practice, and skill level within a discipline is secondary.

The participants who were part of this study are well educated and have a positive gender balance when compared with those of some support group studies. This former point warrants deliberation when one considers the people who may be drawn to and adopt participation in a HOPE group. One might question if the HOPE groups studied here have a healthy representation of males because one guides the groups. These points are worthy of further exploration and deepened understanding to assure that each HOPE group's atmosphere continues to convey welcome to a wide audience.

Study Limitations

Limitations of this study and its design include its retrospective nature and sample size. The design was selected to reflect HOPE's philosophy and acknowledge the restrictions of gathering past clinical information from participants. An increased return of demographic data and HOPE Group Questionnaire would have added value to the descriptive and correlational findings. It is likely that people who chose to participate, particularly in the interview process, have a bias that favors HOPE in particular and support groups in general, thereby influencing the study outcomes. Information regarding involvement with other support groups was gathered anecdotally as part of the interview process. This information may have contributed additional meaning if collected with the demographic data.

Additional limitations include findings that are related to one Guide who is the primary focus, and study design that did not include use of valid and reliable health and quality of life inventories. The groups observed and interviews conducted were with people who had participated in groups guided by Ken Hamilton. This limits the information that is available to assess the outcomes of HOPE's framework when implemented by other Guides. The study design relied on a HOPE-specific inventory and interview content to acquire deepened understanding of HOPE as a framework. This quest necessitated the use of qualitative methods, including those derived from phenomenology, to gather information and insights. The phenomenon of HOPE as experienced by those who have lived it for both brief and long durations, was the focus of interest. The synthesis, analysis, and outcomes of qualitative study would have been enriched by ongoing participation by an additional reviewer.

Directions for Future Research

The promised expansion of HOPE groups in clinical and community settings affords rich research opportunities. These may be Guided-focused and/or participant-focused. The use of prospective designs will permit the examination and synthesis of data to enrich the quantitative as well as qualitative understanding of HOPE over time. Indeed, use of mixed methods designs will contribute greatly to both the breadth and depth of insights realized about HOPE's integration within clinical settings. Research may include selection of health and life quality inventories to measure HOPE's outcomes with new participants. Select clinical indicators may be adopted for research with people who are enrolled in a HOPE clinical group. It is recommended that research strategies that are adopted be non-invasive to align with the safety that HOPE nurtures.

Additional collection of demographic data will contribute to long-term planning for HOPE groups and help to determine who will best benefit from this service. Items to add to a demographic questionnaire include marital/partnering status, occupation, spiritual practice, and income.

HOPE's research base will grow with the inclusion of measures to assess the outcomes and value of Guide preparation, mentoring, and ongoing support. Pre- and post-test methods with design based on HOPE's philosophy and guidelines will contribute to continual refinement of the Guide's role and development.

Part Three: The Practice of HOPE:
A Primer for Practitioners

This portion of the HOPE Story is drawn from the art and science content of the previous sections to present introductory guidance from which to prepare HOPE Guides and develop HOPE Groups. *The HOPE Guide's Manual* (Hamilton, 1996) is the reference for those who engage in the study to become Guides.

This section introduces guidance for the integration and implementation of HOPE Group practice within clinical and community settings. Each presents unique opportunities and challenges for the Guide and group participants. HOPE offers a chance to reduce social isolation as it creates a bridge between clinical care and the business of daily life. Challenges can be as mundane as selecting a day, time, and place to meet. A meeting space may be donated, but does it offer people safety, respect, and ease of access? Fees and reimbursement mechanisms are topics for greater consideration in some settings more than others, yet they are nonetheless considerations that will materialize at some point.

Each setting invites those committed to provide HOPE by fulfilling its promise to immerse in the theoretical framework, thereby creating a thread of continuous care for people from setting to setting. This implies that the commitment to HOPE extends beyond the Guide and participants to the host organization, whether that is a community group or health care agency.

Setting Selection

The term setting selection, when considering HOPE, implies both the type of group and physical location. The type of HOPE Group chosen, based on the model's current evolution, will serve either community-residing people or those receiving care in a clinical setting. In both scenarios it is necessary to select an environment that supports and conveys respect and safety. A setting that is comfortable and cared for, with ease of access to comfort facilities, implies respect for those who frequent the site.

Participants of this study suggested that safety is conveyed by who is present in the group and the personal interactions that manifest. People are able to welcome others with a wide range of needs as long as they feel safety for themselves and for the Guide. This observation asks the HOPE Group that is forming to consider settings in which people will feel safe. Along with this, although the consideration did not arise through either this study or the literature review, is the importance of accessibility for all prospective participants. It is worthy to note that two of the present HOPE meeting sites do offer handicapped accessibility. Other elements that may contribute to safety are lighting, the ability to see who is approaching, a telephone, and onsite or nearby security personnel.

Another element of safety that emerged is one of trust. Some interviewees stated or implied that it is important to trust that other group members will conduct themselves appropriately with each other during and outside of each meeting. Participants stated that the Guide's use of the guidelines throughout a meeting helped to maintain or return to focus. *The Gold Book*, therein, offers gentle and respectful direction for those present.

The Guide Experience

Guide Selection

The Guide trusts and believes that each person has the capacity to find his/her own solutions for meeting life's challenges. The Guide has the ability to recognize the goodness and strength within everybody. Thus the Guide selection process is one that is introspective, intuitive, and relationship-focused. The prospective Guide is asked to reflect on personal qualities and traits that s/he brings to the HOPE experience. These include communication abilities, self-awareness, and relationship-centered awareness. *The HOPE Guide's Manual* (Hamilton, 1996) states that "successful listeners are people who listen intently.... They concentrate on what the other person is saying because they have the intention of hearing [what is said]" (p. 32). Participants repeatedly identified the importance of effective listening, enhanced by an attuned awareness and understanding of body language.

The golden lining of listening and effective communication is silence. It is important for the Guide to be able to sit with silence and support others with doing the same. The ability to hold silence is anchored in reflection and a keen awareness of how this art invites the individual or the group to encounter a source of knowing that arises from thought before expression. It is in the void that one finds authentic voice. The prospective Guide is familiar with this inner terrain and is able to presence the experience for others less acquainted.

The prospective Guide embodies the personal traits of honesty, patience, and gentle kindness. The Guide's personal level of function enfolds the desire to serve with being centered and having confidence in one's own healing. The Guide is actively engaged in the process of personal development and does so with strength, maturity, and courage. HOPE participants and Guides value the ability to "park the ego at the door." Personal authenticity is valued; the person who is comfortable with his/her role demonstrates it.

When relating within the group, the Guide functions non-judgmentally and with resolve and equanimity. S/he presents the principles of attitudinal healing and evokes group cohesion. Meeting flow is an important factor for participants who value the Guide's knowledge of *The Gold Book* and ability to draw on its wisdom to guide dialogue and group interaction. The Guide is described as one who skillfully frames questions and makes reflective comment that invites people to answer their own questions and "do what needs to be done." This presence within the group is gentle and calm and enables the Guide to know who is having a difficult time. Further, the Guide's role is participatory and supports people within the group with active practice of the guidelines. This necessity of participation includes the ability to convey goodness and hope and helps the Guide "to motivate the same in others."

In *The HOPE Guide's Manual* Hamilton (1996) corrects any assumptions that the role of the Guide is one of facilitation.

> Moreover, to call such a guide a 'facilitator' is, for me inappropriate because to 'facilitate' (make easy) is inadequate.... Some people need to enter their own danger waters in order to find their healing. That journey is very difficult and cannot be 'made easy' (p. 30).

Thus the Guide engages in a dance with the individual and the group. This dance evokes a sense of attunement that aligns with right timing. The result is the reflection, word, question, or silent moment that supports another with sourcing personal wisdom.

The intuitive nature of the prospective Guide is revealed by a sense of knowing without an ego-driven need to know. This awareness arises from individual life experience and the Guide values that s/he cannot impart absolute or even partial knowing of another's story or need. The intuitive Guide is one who can support another along the paths of consciousness and personal wisdom, without the need to set direction. This Guide is able to "see the pain behind the behavior" and can do so without owning the problem or attempting to fix it.

Guide Preparation

Prospective Guides agree to participate in a set of HOPE seminars, followed by a period of mentoring and guidance. The first section presents the theoretical foundation and framework of HOPE intertwined with the intricacies of group process. Theory is woven with the experiential practice of sitting in circle, the manner in which HOPE Groups meet. The training participants study the HOPE precepts as they become immersed in active practice of the principles of attitudinal healing. These initial lessons are followed by SoulCircling, an experience that draws the Guide into an exploration of his/her inner life. This circling brings the prospective Guide to the place of transformation in which one can sit in witness of another's shadow and learn from the experience through compassionate awareness rather than through the reactivity of fear or judgment.

The curriculum that encompasses HOPE Guide training is based on the philosophy, principles, and concepts presented in Part One of this book. The key areas of the framework and content for Guide preparation are summarized in Appendix G. The core learning objectives for Guide training are:

As a result of this seminar, participants will:

Describe the role of attitudinal healing in medicine and human care.

Reflect on the Guide's role, qualities, and participation in the HOPE Group experience

Illustrate HOPE Group process and the purpose and functions of *The Gold Book*

The HOPE Group: Form and Function

Group Members

HOPE can be viewed as an invitation, something offered out of respect, care, or love to another human. HOPE calls to and has meaning for people with a range of needs from many life paths and circumstances. Each one comes to HOPE in search of new options for meeting that which life is presenting them. Some arrive having been in support groups for years, or on and off. Reaching out for support is a new experience for others. Taking the step to enter a group may be tentative at best. Some people seek out HOPE at the behest of a loved one who then shares the experience for some period of time. Others arrive at HOPE because their physician made the suggestion.

The thing that people have in common is that each individual chose to give HOPE a try. The next choice they made was to continue. Even for those who attend once, or a few times, not to return, the value lies in the act of making their own choice. In the interviews, more than one participant said that a person needs to be ready for HOPE and really, only that person knows if s/he is in that state of readiness. That knowing may not be clear for many weeks of sitting in a HOPE meeting. HOPErs' comments revealed that when that knowing arises it is heart-centered. HOPE becomes something that one carries into and through life. Years after their last meeting, many continue to draw on the strength found within *The Gold Book*.

Group Process

The circle, a ring of chairs, symbolizes equanimity and the ever-present flow of life. The door opens and HOPE enters. HOPE is of many ages yet ageless, of many faces yet with common expression, and is renewed by each person who embraces its concepts and gifts. There are quiet glances of recognition, a seat selected, a parcel placed on the floor. More people enter and one person passes around the goldenrod laminated flyers. This, *The Gold Book*, is held tenderly. The HOPE meeting begins... "We are a H.O.P.E. Group..." Each person reads in turn, the words flowing clockwise round the circle. Some read, others recite; they carry the words in their hearts.

Some meetings begin with a person who has need to speak and does so, finding comfort by sharing words carried there for others to hear. At other meetings the beginning moments are quiet. The silence is filled with a palpable gratitude for the time together, no matter what it holds. For it may mean sitting with another's grief and heartache that their load might be somewhat lightened because other people care enough to listen.

As a person speaks, some watch intently and others cast their gaze to the floor. Some lean forward, others slid loosely on their chairs. But everyone listens. Each person there knows that when it is her/his turn, people will listen. That's how it is in a HOPE Group.

The two hours pass and it is time to close. Everyone gathers in a circle and holds hands, "Life, grant me the serenity..."

The HOPE Group process springs directly from *The Gold Book*. It too is solidly guided by the words written there. Each line shares a key for shifting one's attitude, for transforming one's life. The points of the HOPE Group Opening serve as elements for contemplation both during the meeting and in quiet moments.

"We come together." HOPE conveys unity and people who attend regularly know that their presence is held when they miss a meeting. "Wellness comes with the discovery of peace of mind." The implication is that wellness and peace of mind are linked and the latter is not a given. It is something to be discovered, and though one may search on one's own, others who have traversed the inner landscape can guide the search.

"We choose to focus on the whole of life." People find that which describes wholeness for them. The Guide, or another group member, asks a question or makes a reflective statement to prompt thought. As one person searches for wholeness and what life might hold with its realization, others in the group reflect on their own perceptions of its meaning. There are lessons that emerge from others' stories. HOPE fosters an environment that cultivates the dance between group process and personal reflection.

The Principles of Attitudinal Healing contribute to the tone of how one can interact with him/herself and others throughout life. Each one of the twelve statements is a study unto itself about the art of being human. The joys and travails that life can bring are covered in a modest number of words; being, love, peace, health, fear, giving, receiving, forgiving, judging, faultfinding, perceptions, death, and calling for love.

The HOPE Group Guidelines set forth ten agreements. These set the tone for interaction with one's self and with others. There are elements of civility and decency. They convey respect for each person's process and contributions. Each person comes with something to learn, each person has something to share, and each person leaves enriched by the presence of self within the group.

Part Four: The Heart of HOPE—its Stories

This book opened with the Story of HOPE as one person's inspiration that became a theoretical framework from which to guide the care of thousands of people who were seeking comfort. HOPE's story relates to an organization that embodies a way of caring for people that honors all comers, any ailment, and the joys and miracles that may happen along life's journey.

This book closes with stories of people whose lives HOPE did touch and who have extended HOPE to others. Each is presented to give you, the reader, as a glimpse into the 'once told tale' of several HOPErs. Each is told through the author's voice, reflectively weaving each person's words through the gift of story.

This section of the HOPE story is dedicated to the art of care. It calls to the heart of the matter, that being each person's value and experience that emerges through that which we call life. As you read each story, please think of your own. What words and messages would be on these pages, were this your story? How do any of these messages stir something within you that mirrors your personal wisdom? If something happened to you or loved one that caused you to have to meet life head-on, what relationships and voices would bring you love in those most difficult of times?

Each person here is identified by pseudonym and her/his story is related in a way to honor privacy. Each story is published with the permission of the individual author.

Therese

Therese previously had cancer and felt healed after a complicated round of chemotherapy. She met Ken at a conference and "had an interesting conversation with him." "I had been through one cancer experience without HOPE in my twenties. I had a husband and a young child. Then I was diagnosed again. I started going to HOPE and I took an active part in healing with hope. And I tried to be grateful."

Therese spoke of how she learned from others. Hearing their stories and witnessing how people were living their lives, caused her to open to "things to do about the mindbody from within.... There were so many healing things that I learned." "I really felt every week that I could go to a place where I could listen to others and speak and be there in a non-judgmental way. And it was healing all parts of my life not just the disease. I learned more through listening to others. I really liked the visualization and meditation and used them outside the meeting."

Therese attended HOPE meetings regularly for three years. "In HOPE I learned to rely on my internal resources and myself for healing." She has carried HOPE with her in the years since she participated in meetings. "HOPE became a part of who I am." In recent years, Therese and her family moved back to the town where she grew up. Cancer returned and this time was diagnosed at an earlier stage than in the past. Therese knew there was no HOPE group in her area. "I realized I didn't need to go to a HOPE group this time. I worked on it on my own... with prayer and meditation and visualization."

Therese tells her story with heart-centered depth. Her tone of voice conveys the gratitude she feels. "I have used HOPE for many situations in my life. Awareness of choices and of how to look at things [in another way] were gifts from HOPE." She speaks about balance and life changes and making the time to be present to life. "I became more aware of a balance in my life. I had always felt balanced but now really knew the importance of nature and of seeing a butterfly... making those times a priority."

Tom

Tom was a young man when he had a heart attack. He went to HOPE for his wife, "I did it to make her happy." That was over a decade ago. Tom is pretty clear about what he believes HOPE did for him. "Honestly believe I wouldn't be here without Ken and HOPE. I had all I could do to go up the steps at the HOPE Center."

There are five steps that lead up to the HOPE Center front door. Tom ascended those steps regularly for six years and still pops in every once in a while. He has reasons to do so. "Here I am and I have a great attitude. I was completely hyper and now I am calm. I could go on and on about HOPE. I learned so much from other people. I made friends with people who had cancer and AIDS and they knew they only had a few months to live and they were smiling."

Tom has experienced loss and triumph over the years since he first attended HOPE. His beloved wife died a number of years ago. Despite this Tom states he has a positive attitude. "One of the greatest things I learned from Ken was to look at everything from a positive side. If not, you'll be sick and depressed and no good to yourself or others.... The key is the positive attitude. I surround myself with friends who have a good outlook."

A few years after the heart attack, Tom recalls that "I had a test of my heart. After the heart attack only 1/3 of my heart was working because of the damage to the muscle. Some of the veins had started working again and they said to me, 'that's not supposed to happen.'"

Tom has shared his "positive energy" with other people who were gravely ill and dying. He finds meaning in sharing what he learned through HOPE one on one with people. His voice is clear and his message about the value of HOPE is solid, "I'm talking to you from the voice of experience."

Hugh

Hugh has been an active HOPE participant for several years. Hugh came to HOPE after finding himself on the receiving end of criminal hate. He has attended HOPE and other support groups to move beyond trauma and create an opening for "self-forgiveness, catharsis, and purging of cultural ideas given to me."

Hugh finds HOPE and the people who belong to the group intellectually stimulating. These factors contribute appreciably to his place in the world. "HOPE acts as a compass—I need direction. I hear it in different stories. When I get that feeling I need to work on [something].... It's a sense of community for me. I've done a lot of work on myself—it's like topsoil to fortify what I have already built."

HOPE has influenced Hugh's life in other ways. I have a "tremendous amount of tolerance and patience with others [and] an appreciation for my surroundings and the magical and simple things." The magic happens for Hugh as each meeting unfolds according to the day and who is present. Likewise, he is keenly aware of his own place within the group and that his presence is a gift for others. "If I weren't there I'd be missed by someone and I know it."

Hugh is drawn to story and delights in the mythology that emerges from each person's circumstances when one looks beyond perceptions to seek meaning. "HOPE has launched me into mythology reading and watching Joseph Campbell. He's my #1 man. Our genetic memory for the hunt—it is in our hearts and becomes physically translated. Because of the 12-step program and HOPE and mythology I live with little confusion today."

"HOPE focuses on the whole person and identifies the whole as therapeutic." Hugh describes the HOPE process in words that connote vitality and action. "You walk into life when you walk into HOPE and life happens." This quality of dynamism and expansion becomes a rooted experience as one continues to engage within this community of support. "You grow better when you stay where you are planted and get your legs under you and you are willing to challenge yourself." Hugh's voice is quietly sincere as he reflects on how HOPE has contributed to his life story. "For the first time in my life I am following my dreams."

Beth

Beth's HOPE Group participation extends back almost one year. The physician who is treating her for an inflammatory condition told her about HOPE. Beth's words resonate the depth of meaning that a person can find within a HOPE setting. "I have felt very strongly about the HOPE group since my second time coming. I try to attend weekly as possible, and have missed maybe only around five since [early in the year]. I wish I had come sooner. I value the people who tend to come regularly and even if I don't speak or ask advice, I'm interested in and learn from others. It serves to make me think—which I like."

Beth's story is distinctly and uniquely her own, yet holds common threads with people over the last two decades who have found a community of support within a HOPE group. Her words are reflective of someone with a new diagnosis and the myriad emotions associated with significant life events. "It allowed me to cry and vent my misery (and continues to do so) and get very needed validation... it was all right to cry. I needed to get so much out that was inside of me, and that it had been stored up and festering for many months. I slowly discharged these negative feelings/thoughts while at the group and I cried less at other times, thank god!"

Beth is very reflective about her experiences within the HOPE group and credits the group with her own opening and expanded view of life circumstances. "The group initiated questions for me... and made me even (I think) more open-minded about many possibilities and perceptions. Maybe most importantly, it allowed me to realize that good health does not necessarily mean without sickness and that it is possible to have an illness and still be emotionally healthy."

Beth experienced some remission in the disease process and was able to return to work. "The group allowed me to move through, as I could, my illness, depression, and anxiety; it helped me to start feeling a bit of confidence that I could, maybe, just maybe, work again.... I feel I was able to get a job and start working because of my experience in the HOPE group."

Beth clearly describes how the HOPE focus adds to its value as a support group. "Focus on the positive without ignoring the negative—there are no shoulds. So one can get validation and support, vent and be turned toward the prospect of hopefulness—that it is possible in all situations. It is not a psychoeducational group and yet gives much information and allows the ability to learn from Ken and others. It does not focus on what not to do, and to celebrate and appreciate whatever we can."

Judy

Judy relates that she first learned about HOPE after she had attended several sessions of counseling through her workplace. She has been attending a HOPE group for just over two years and is quite certain that "it's the best thing that's ever happened to me." Judy describes her life as one based on rejection and relates how HOPE has supported her with feelings of abandonment. Because of this it has "helped to validate my past... HOPE allows me to be me, not something I am not."

Judy had experience with group work prior to her time with HOPE. "I've done a lot of healing work and group things in the past. I came with complete knowledge of what I needed; have been doing this a long time—started the questioning thirty years ago." Despite the time and energy Judy has devoted to personal development, she feels there is more to do and wishes to have continued support with her growth. "I need a spirit-centered life.... I'm afraid not to come back. If it's working, what will happen if not?"

When asked how HOPE has influenced her life, Judy responds "HOPE is more intimate because it is smaller. The guidelines bring the differences to the front; they help to provide focus. It attracts me. I need a little social life. But I do it mostly for guidance and to apply to everyday life." Judy applies the guidance by showing compassion for her former husband who is dying. "It's taken me thirty years to line up the head and the heart. I want to be healthy and happy and to make up for the past."

HOPE has encouraged Judy with "health changes that are emotional. I am more in tune with what I am saying and not overreacting." She thinks back to when she first attended HOPE and what she hoped to gain from her experience. "Mine was to seek inner peace; to have respect and dignity and loving yourself. I just want to live in the moment. Hope has allowed me to forgive myself. I can see the beauty in simple things. Allowing myself some pleasures... and learning to have fun and relax. That's the hardest thing for me to do."

<hr />

Ken's Story

This story neither uses a pseudonym nor in any way protects its subject; for this is Ken's Story, a synthesis of reflections and quotations that speak of his qualities, his humanity, and his mastery of the "once told tale."

Ken describes how his work with HOPE has profoundly affected his life. "Stories of abuse brought me into a listening space." From that space where some not only witness but also feel the suffering of another human, Ken began his deep exploration into Earl Nightingale's work.

It's absolutely necessary here to talk about some of Ken's personal traits and attributes. He possesses a sharp intellect that is enwrapped by an encyclopedic memory. Many people commented on this during the interviews. Use of these skills is one way in which the HOPE meetings stay fresh and vibrant. And, as one person pointed out, his presentation of the latest-read book is much more than a review. The book is illustrated with language and demeanor that relate passion and excitement and a storyteller's ability to tie meaning with those of other sources.

Ken acknowledges the pain, suffering, growth, and joy of others because he does the same for himself. He has learned to share his own mystery and metaphor with people in groups, or who visit with him in his practice, that they may gain insights into their own stories by hearing his. Ken's voice is soft and low, with a timber that is rehearsed and real in the same breath. His gaze tends to be lively, given energy by his love for people and the often hauntingly rich experiences he has shared with them.

Ken has the hands of a surgeon, a master craftsman, and one who stacks wood to prepare for a Maine winter. He uses these hands that have touched so many to put words on a page. This is the experience of the glider pilot mind gathering poetic phrases to bring hope and meaning to utterances in the void or symbolic form to paper. It is the wisdom of the shaman who crafts canoes of wood to navigate Maine's waters and boats of hide to traverse the spirit realms. It is the precision of the surgeon who once opened peoples' bodies to help them heal, and now guides them to open to the healing of the Self.

These words are written symbolically to paint the picture of a life that is lived in mythic proportions. That is how Ken lives. Each day brings new color and the constant reminder that there is more to do to bring peace to the human experience. His work is suited only for those who have courage: the courage to be authentic; the courage to persevere; and, the courage to be kind, even in the face of challenge.

This is the human form that gave life to HOPE. But Ken might dispute that, for HOPE came to him. It chose him when he had no choice but to bow to its power and grace. HOPE presents each person with the challenge to live out his or her unique gifts each and every day. Ken describes the loving action this process embodies, "HOPE does not attach, does not put shoulds on them. Being able to detach from the outcome and be present to the person and watching them move on." A favorite mantram of his is the title of a Sam Walter Foss (1858-1911) poem, "Let me live in a house by the side of the road and be a friend to man."

He has watched and listened to people who, even in the midst of significant illness, want to focus on something beyond the problem. "HOPE doesn't focus on handling the problem... it sees it as a springboard for the rest of your life. In a disease-focused group you get a lot of information. HOPE asks, 'Now what are you going to do with your life?'" Ken has learned that meeting people with the potential of hope brings meaning and the gift of renewal, even when their days here are few.

Ken was open about challenges because they exist. One is "being able to ride and be patient with a situation" and another is "the failure of this to happen and have my own personal sense of disappointment with it." Some challenges are "big" and are beyond HOPE's supportive reach. Yet that is part of the human condition; a part about which there are so many lessons.

This is how he has carried out his interpretation and message of Nightingale's work... to succeed, one focuses on that which gives meaning to her or his life. Ken focused on finding hope for his patients and HOPE sought him out. Together, Ken and HOPE have held forth a symbol that is a gift for those who choose to seek meaning, value and purpose in their life.

For Ken, his contributions to HOPE have been a large piece of his life's work; so we end with the opening quote (p. xi) as a fitting closure of the circle of HOPE: "It has been an absolutely wonderful delight, honor, and privilege to serve people in this way; and they have helped me appreciate my role as one who sees the value of being human."

References

Adamsen, L., & Rasmussen, J. M. (2003). Exploring and encouraging through social interaction: A qualitative study of nurses' participation in self-help groups for cancer patients. *Cancer Nursing, 26*(1), 28-36.

Arthur, A. R., & Edwards, C. (2005). An evaluation of support groups for patients with long-term chronic pain and complex psychosocial difficulties. *European Journal of Psychotherapy, Counselling and Health, 7*(3), 169-180.

"attitudinal healing" (2006) http://www.attitudinalhealing.org/

BKWSU, Brahma Kumaris World Spiritual University, http://www.thoughtfortoday.org.uk/

Bohm, D. (2002) *Wholeness and the implicate order.* London: Routledge.

Brophy, T., Skillings, A., & Chandler, J. (1991). *HOPE: A community filled with love.* Unpublished manuscript, Portland: University of Southern Maine.

Brown, A. E., Whitney, S. N., Schneider, M. A., & Vega, C. P. (2006). Alcohol recovery and spirituality: Strangers, friends, and partners? *Southern Medical Journal, 99*(6), 654-657.

Burns, N., & Grove, S. K. (2001). *The practice of nursing research: Conduct, critique, and utilization,*(4th ed.). Philadelphia: W. B. Saunders Company.

Capra, F. (1996). *The web of life: A new scientific understanding of living systems.* New York: Anchor Books.

Cassell, E. (2004). *The nature of suffering and the goals of medicine.* New York: Oxford.

Coward, D. D. (2005). Lessons learned in developing a support intervention for African American women with breast cancer. *Oncology Nursing Forum 32*(2), 261-266.

Dadich, A. (2006). Self-help support groups: Adding to the toolbox of mental health care options for young men. *Youth Studies Australia, 25*(1), 33-40.

Frankl, V. (1992). *Man's search for meaning.* Boston: Beacon.

Grande, G. E., Myers, L. B., & Sutton, S. R. (2005). How do patients who participate in cancer support groups differ from those who do not? *Psycho-Oncology, 15,* 321-334.

Hamilton, K. H. (1993). *The gold book.* South Paris, Maine: HOPE Healing Publications.

Hamilton, K. H. (1996). *The HOPE guide's manual.* South Paris, Maine: Hope Healing Publications.

Hamilton, K. H. (2005). *White paper on HOPE groups and HOPE guiding.* South Paris, Maine: Hope Healing Publications.

Hill, N. (1937). *Think and grow rich.* Northbrook, IL: The Napoleon Hill Foundation.

H.O.P.E., Incorporated. (1998). *HOPE survey for HOPE guides, guide trainees, and Circling the Soul participants.* South Paris ME: Author.

Knight, C. (2006). Groups for individuals with traumatic histories: Practice considerations for social workers. *Social Work, 51*(1), 20-30.

Lampropoulos, G. K., & Spengler, P. M. (2005). Helping and change without traditional therapy: Commonalities and opportunities. *Counseling Psychology Quarterly, 18*(1), 47-59.

Leung, J., & Arthur, D. G. (2004). Clients and facilitators' experiences of participating in a Hong Kong self-help group for people recovering from mental illness. *International Journal of Mental Health Nursing,13,* 232-241.

Moody, R. (1992). *Life after life.* Harrisburg: Stackpole.

Nightingale-Conant. (2006). Retrieved October 18, 2006 from http://www.nightingale.com/tWWW_Main.asp

Nightingale, E. (1996). *The strangest secret.* Keys Publishing, http://www.nightingaleproducts.com.

Norcross, J. C., Hedges, M., & Prochaska, J. O. (2002). The face of 2010: A delphi poll on the future of psychotherapy. *Professional Psychology: Research and Practice, 33*(3), 316-322.

Palmer, P. (1997). *The courage to teach.* San Francisco: Jossey-Bass.

Paquet, M., Bolduc, N., Xhignesse, M., & Vanasse, A. (2005). Re-engineering cardiac rehabilitation programmes: Considering the patient's point of view. *Journal of Advanced Nursing, 51*(6), 567-576.

Pitkala, K. H., Blomquist, L., Routasalo, P., Saarenheimo, M., Karvinen, E., & Oikarinen, U., et al. (2004). Leading groups of older people: A description and evaluation of the education of professionals. *Educational Gerontology, 30,* 821-833.

Pories, S., Jain, S., & Harper, G. (Eds.) (2006).*The soul of a doctor.* Chapel Hill: Algonquin.

Ring, K. (1984). *Heading toward omega.* New York: William Morrow.

Ruffolo, M. C., Kuhn, M. T., & Evans, M. E. (2006). Developing a parent-professional team leadership model in group work: Work with families with children experiencing behavioral and emotional problems. *Social Work, 51*(1), 39-47.

Sheldrake, R. (1988). *The presence of the past: morphic resonance and the habits of nature.* New York: Crown.

Symynkywicz, J. (1991). Vaclav Havel and the politics of hope. *Noetic Sciences Review,* 18, 21.

Tatton, G. (1997). *HOPE member survey.* Unpublished manuscript.

Tolle, E. (2001).*The power of now..* Novato, CA: New World.

Tracy, B. (1987). *The psychology of achievement.* Chicago: Nightingale-Conant.

U. S. Bureau State and County Quick Facts. (2006). Retrieved November 15, 2006 from http://quickfacts.census.gov/qfd/states/23000.html

Walch, S. E., Roetzer, L. M., & Minnett, T. A. (2006). Support group participation among persons with HIV: Demographic characteristics and perceived barriers. *AIDS Care, 18*(4), 284-289.

Zabalegui, A., Sanchez, S., Sanchez, P. D., & Juando, C. (2005). Nursing and cancer support groups. *Journal of Advanced Nursing, 51*(4), 369-381.

Ziegler, L., Smith, P. A., & Fawcett, J. (2004). Breast cancer:
      Evaluation of the Common Journey Breast Cancer Support
      Group. *Journal of Clinical Nursing, 13*(4), 467-478.

Appendix A

The HOPE Group Project: HOPE Group Questionnaire

Consultant for the Study: Joyce O. Murphy RN, MSN, AHN-BC
Source: This study is being conducted by HOPE.

Purpose: This study is designed to expand on the present base of knowledge about HOPE Groups. Information that is gathered will help HOPE to learn more about the ways in which group participation contributes to peoples' lives and the manner in which each Guide influences a group's relationships.

Assurances of confidentiality: The information that is collected is confidential and has been reviewed and approved by the HOPE Board of Directors. The following information will be used to generally describe the group of people who participate in HOPE Groups. Each individual's identity and personal information will be protected by assurances of confidentiality.

Demographic Data

Information from this section will be used to compare participants enrolled in this study with those presented in the professional medical literature about support groups.

1. Personal information: Please check those that apply.
    Gender: Male _____ Female _____
    Age Range: 20-29 __ 30-39 __ 40-49 __ 50-59 __ 60+ __

2. County of residence _____

3. Educational information: Please check those that apply.

High School/GED _____ Some college _____
Bachelor's degree _____ Master's degree or higher _____

4. HOPE Group participation: Please answer the following—
    approximations are welcome!
    a. I have attended meetings from (month and year) _____
        to (month and year) _____
    b. I have attended approximately ___HOPE Group meetings.
    c. I have attended _____HOPE Groups in this location (s):
                              Thank You!

Appendix B

Level of Agreement Questionnaire

This questionnaire is part of a study being conducted to learn more
about HOPE Groups and the value they have in peoples' lives. We
are asking for your opinion because we hold your participation in
HOPE Groups in high regard. Your responses will be treated with
respect and confidentiality. Participants' responses will be presented
only as group information in writing or discussion.
Please respond to the following statements by indicating your level
of agreement with each.

Strongly disagree: 1, Disagree:2, Agree:3, Strongly agree:4

1. Wellness comes with the discovery of peace of mind.
        1   2   3   4
2. We come to realize that the power that makes choice possible
    lies within each one of us.
        1   2   3   4
3. With love's power we come to realize the promise of HOPE
        1   2   3   4
4. HOPE groups focus on health and healing through the power of
    HOPE to open doors otherwise closed by fear.

     1   2   3   4
5. Finding a state of 'inner peace' is easy.
     1   2   3   4
6. HOPE group participation supports people to move from fear and anger to happiness and joy.
     1   2   3   4
7. Health is a wholeness of self.
     1   2   3   4
8. My participation in HOPE Group meetings transformed my attitude about my health.
     1   2   3   4
9. Health is the absence of disease.
     1   2   3   4
10. Participating in HOPE Group meetings has changed my understanding of the meaning of my life.
     1   2   3   4

Please indicate level of agreement with the following statements about the HOPE Group Guide's role during meetings.

The HOPE Guide conducts meetings in a manner that:

1. Helps the group focus on attitudinal healing by seeing life in a peaceful and loving way.
     1   2   3   4
2. Recognizes the importance of each person's process thereby creating a safe atmosphere for the whole group.
     1   2   3   4
3. Uses our time together with mutual care, consideration, and respect.
     1   2   3   4
4. Limits the sharing of her/his own personal experience.
     1   2   3   4
5. Maintains a loving focus on each speaker.
     1   2   3   4

Appendix C

HOPE Group Observation Guidelines

HOPE Group observations will be conducted with attention to the phenomena occurring during each meeting. The process will be reflective in nature, deriving the foundation of the phenomenological observations from HOPE materials. These include *The HOPE Guide's Manual, The Golden Book, All About HOPE, and The White Paper on HOPE.*

Observations of individual participants will be de-identified. Observations of the Guide, including verbal comment, will be noted. Observation will include pacing as well as the following components drawn from the resources noted above. Notes from the meeting will be transcribed and analyzed for content that is inclusive of concepts, communication patterns, and quality of interaction as it compares with that suggested in the HOPE materials.

Meeting Ritual

- Opening
    - The questions:
        - "Who are you?"
        - "Why are you here?"
        - "How are you going to get what you came for?"
        - "What are you going to do with it when you have it?"
    - The affirmations
    - The guidelines
    - Introduction of new persons
    - Sharing by experienced members
- Closing
    - Use of imagery, song, or affirmations
    - A Prayer for Serenity

Meeting Guidelines

- Confidentiality; no records are kept
- "The agenda walks in through the door."
  Communication Guidelines
- Honor time commitments,
- Focus on the one who is speaking,
- See others in a loving way,
- Share what works for us, and
- Risk and expose our own emotional states.
  Guide conduct
- S/he practices and models listening skills that include the ability to:
    o Listen with open heart and mind,
    o Ask open, honest questions for clarification and deeper understanding,
    o Avoid criticizing or advice-giving,
    o Affirm people for their experience in meeting life's circumstances,
    o Encourage them to create benefit for self and others from that experience, and
    o Display the following in practice:
        - Repression of one's own ego,
        - Patience,
        - Concern,
        - The ability to reflect, and
        - The ability to affirm another person's qualities.
- The Guide's role in communication includes:
    o Active non-judgmental participation in group process,
    o The use of silence as a form of speech,
    o The role of a communication coach who:
        - Encourages communication methods,

- Guides to development and practice of helpful attitudes, and
- Encourages participants to practice goal setting and the use of imagination in their lives.
  o Providing support to understand a person's problem by:
    - Guiding a person to focus on the meaning and possibilities that life contains and which lie beyond the problem, and encouraging anyone who needs conventional therapy to find it outside the group.

Appendix D

HOPE Group Participant Interview Guidelines

Guidelines for participant interviews are derived from *The HOPE Guide's Manual* and *The HOPE White Paper*. The conduct of interviews is intended to follow the communication principles supported by HOPE. These include active listening, non-judgmental awareness, and appreciation for each person's story and participation in HOPE Groups. The interviewer will take notes and use these to contribute to the content analysis of all interviews that are conducted. Confidentiality is assured according to adherence with human subjects protection and the completed consent form. The following questions and statements will guide the interview process:

- How did you learn about HOPE Groups?
- Please share why you chose to participate in HOPE Group meetings.
- It is important for us, through this study, to consider the ways in which HOPE Group participation affects people. Please describe

the ways in which the HOPE Group you attend (ed) has influenced your life.

- Describe what you value the most about your HOPE Group experience.
  - o Will you relate one particular experience that was particularly meaningful or fulfilling for you?
  - o Positive life changes can happen for many reasons. Please relate one way in which HOPE contributed to positive changes in your life story.
- HOPE's view of the role of supportive groups is extraordinary. What is your perception about the ways in which HOPE differs from other groups?
- Please describe what you feel is the most important quality a person needs to be a HOPE Guide.
- If you have not yet completed a HOPE participant question-naire, you are invited to do so
- If not answered above:
  - What changes have you made in your life as a result of participating in HOPE?
- If you care to share the following information, it will help the study with information analysis:
  - o The HOPE Group that you attended,
  - o Your approximate dates of attendance, and
  - o How frequently you attended HOPE Group meetings.

Appendix E

HOPE Group Guide Interview Guidelines

Guidelines for guide interviews are derived from *The HOPE Guide's Manual* and *The HOPE White Paper*. The conduct of interviews is intended to follow the communication principles supported by HOPE. These include active listening, non-judgmental awareness, and appreciation for each person's story regarding HOPE Groups.

The interviewer will take notes and use these to contribute to the content analysis of all interviews that are conducted. Confidentiality is assured according to adherence with human subjects protection and the completed consent form. People who volunteer to participate in the interview process will receive the following list of topics prior to their interview in order to have time to reflect on and prepare their responses.

The following questions and statements will guide the interview process:

- How did you learn about HOPE Groups?
- Please share why you chose to become a HOPE Group Guide.
- It is important for us, through this study, to consider the ways in which HOPE Group participation affects people. Please describe the ways in which the HOPE Group you guide (d) has influenced your life.
- Describe what you value the most about your HOPE Group experience.
    o Will you relate one particular experience that was particularly meaningful or fulfilling for you?
    o Positive life changes can happen for many reasons. Please relate one way in which HOPE contributed to positive changes in your life story.
- HOPE's view of the role of supportive groups is extraordinary.
    o What is your perception about the ways in which HOPE differs from other groups?
    o Describe the ways in which you as a guide cultivate the extraordinary nature of HOPE.
- Please describe the qualities you brought to the role of HOPE Guide.
    o Please share those qualities that you have gained or enriched upon because of your experience as a HOPE guide.
    o What qualities do you believe to be absolutely essential for a person to become a HOPE Group Guide?

Appendix F

HOPE Guide Qualities

1) <u>According to the Guide's Manual</u> (Quotes from pp. 39-40)
    a) Communication Skills (2)
        i)   Assumes the responsibility for holding the group to the context of *The Gold Book*
        ii) Is a non-judgmental, active listener who reflects and affirms each person's story
    b) Self-awareness (7)
        i)   Personal traits
            (I) Has personal qualities of compassion and insight
            (II) Must be physically, emotionally, mentally, and spiritually sound,
        ii) Level of function
            (I)   Is open-hearted and courageous, trusting self and the group to hold truth in a safe container
            (II) Actively participates in the group with her or his own process
            (III) Shares her or his own emotional states
        iii) Qualities of Transcendence
            (I) Is peaceful, centered, and present to perceptions, no matter how dark
            (II) Agrees to let go of any need for analysis and to focus instead on synthesis
    c) Relationship-centered Awareness * (9)
        i)   Personal traits
            (I) Is a catalyst, not a helper or enabler
            (II) Practices openness, trustworthiness and honesty
        ii) Level of function
            (I) "Guides the traveler through the rapids by kind and loving means"
            (II) Must not try to help the butterfly out of the chrysalis

   (III) Is an active defender of the right of all HOPErs to
    feel safe

   (IV) Follows the principle, "First, do no harm."
    (Paraphrased)

  iii) Qualities of Transcendence

   (I) Trusts that group members are capable of finding
    their own solutions

   (II) Is loving, caring, and forgiving

   (III) Recognizes the basic goodness and strength within
    each group member

2) According to Interviewed Guides (n=6)

 a) Communication Skills (6)

  i) Use of 'I' statements and choices and attitude

  ii) Just don't use advice giving or 'do so as...'

  iii) Be the queen of questions for clarifying

  iv) Refocusing

  v) Listening Attributes

   (I) Open to listening

   (II) Needs to listen and be quiet.

 b) Self-awareness (11)

  i) Personal traits

   (I) Patient

   (II) Courage

   (III) Gentle

  ii) Level of function

   (I) A desire to be of service to others

   (II) Confidence in one's own healing

   (III) Well grounded and maintain center

   (IV) Park ego at the door

  iii) Qualities of Transcendence

   (I) Maintain guidelines without personal judgment—
    each Guide has things triggered by his/her own stuff

   (II) Accept your own unfoldment when it takes place

           (III)   Intuition—is it used ethically and responsibly, not invading someone else's stuff by really probing... that's coming from the ego

           (IV)   Person needs to have some kind of healing experience... personally

c)   Relationship-centered Awareness (17)

  i)   Personal traits

      (I)   A broad background of books read for stimulation.

      (II)   Need to be able to get down to street level

  ii)   Level of function

      (I)   A lay person... you don't see the text book... to step out of the role.

      (II)   Caring

      (III)   Sensitive

      (IV)   People's stuff comes up

      (V)   Non-judgmental

      (VI)   Won't invoke the part about knowing

      (VII)   Help them to learn the principles of attitudinal healing.

      (VIII)   Help them to go to a psychiatrist/counselor when needed.

  iii)   Qualities of Transcendence

      (I)   Love

      (II)   Compassion

      (III)   Focuses on the present and the whole rather that the fragments

      (IV)   Knowing you can't change the world... but hopefully you can alter one thing

      (V)   Let them do their own healing.

      (VI)   They are looking for something and need to be heard.

3)   According to Interviewed Participants (n=25)

  a)   Communication Skills (13)

    i)   Listening Attributes mentioned 10 times

(I) Wonderful listening skills
(II) Good listening
(III) A good listener.
(IV) Able to listen.
(V)   Active listening
(VI) Good listener
(VII) Listening with love
(VIII) Good listener
(IX) Listening and, most importantly, hearing
(X)   Providing positive feedback and listening
ii) Awareness of body language; this comment and:
(I)   Know and read body language
iii) Humor
b) Self-awareness (38)
i) Personal traits
(I)   Need to be strong.
(II)   Patience: mentioned twice
(III) Relaxed and calm: stated three times
(IV)   Responsible
(V)   Kindness
(VI)   Objectivity
(VII) Honesty
(VIII) Open
(IX)   Experience; some age (stated twice) in actual years
(X)   Need five years of maturity—need to have been in a circle somewhere doing something.
(XI)   To have gone through grief and come out on the other side
(XII) Education
(01) Well read
(XIII) Have a good feeling about themselves
(XIV) Full of peace... a passionate peace.
ii) Level of function
(I)   Anyone can if they want to enough.

      (II)   Intuitive

      (III) Inner strength—ego goes away

      (IV) To be completely themselves at this.

      (V)   Be excited and animated about experiencing the 'now'

      (VI) Be aware there is no such thing as an expert

      (VII) The number one key is a positive outlook and attitude.

      (VIII) Comfortable that he's in the right place

  iii) Qualities of Transcendence

      (I) To come more from a space of love and gratitude and not there to rescue.

      (II)   Depth and spiritual wisdom

      (III) Wisdom stated three times

      (IV) Spirituality

      (V)   People who are centered and balanced in their own life and able to focus on others.

      (VI) To have respect and dignity and loving yourself.

      (VII) A very deep center and strong anchor in knowing who they are. They can't be there because they need help.

      (VIII) They need to be far along on the path... be there for the ones coming without needing anything.

      (IX) Have the ego in the service of the soul.

c) Relationship-centered Awareness (52)

  i) Personal traits

      (I)   Better guides if they have been involved at the participant level.

      (II)   Have psychology training beyond the high school level.

      (III) To have some level of understanding of people.

      (IV) To have a good memory as a guide.

      (V)   Is embracing of the concepts of the HOPE organization.

(VI) Understands group process.

(VII) Not to be stuffy

(VIII) Doing some of the reference [? Referral] work

(IX) Understanding and first hand experience in health care

(X)   An alternative approach

ii) Level of function

(I) Nonjudgmental: stated five times; and—not sitting in some pious righteousness.

(II)   Empathy

(III) Equanimity—sees all equal

(IV) Resolve: I can trust someone when I know they'll be there

(V)   Sense of permanence—I want an icon.

(VI) Can't impose their will on the people in the group

(VII) Support

(VIII) Need to be able to evoke cohesiveness

(IX)   Won't try to give advice mentioned twice

(X)   Regarding meeting flow

(01) Work the group so they don't monopolize.

(02) No agenda—can be hard when the guide is a clinician.

(03) Guiding discussions

(04) Being able to 'hold' the meeting at certain moments

(05) Facilitates in a way that allows you to answer your own questions.

(06) A good way of being with people and bringing them back and using *The Gold Book* to do so... it really helps.

(07) Can take in what everyone is saying...

(08) Knowing *The Gold Book*.

(09) To be a facilitator who enables others to do what needs to be done.

iii) Qualities of Transcendence
   (I) Basing it on love and knowing what questions to ask
        and being open and non-judgmental.
   (II) Helps others with what they need to say.
   (III) Someone with tremendous love and who is
        inclusive, no exceptions, not even for ~
   (IV) Can see the pain behind the behavior.
   (V) Draws people out without doing so in a prying
        manner
   (VI) With those who couldn't be helped but be
        compassionate and openhearted.
   (VII) Ability to see and think of goodness, positiveness,
        and HOPE. Be able to motivate the same in others
   (VIII) Compassion and healing compassion
   (IX) A gentleness in leading the group and participating
        in the group is a necessity
   (X) Know who's having a difficult time
   (XI) Calm in how they handle any situation
   (XII) Knows how to acknowledge when people are really
        down... that's not who they are... not judging. That
        would make the person feel worse.
   (XIII) Someone who often can, after listening, would
        ask a question that causes me to look inside
   (XIV) Be in a relaxed atmosphere... the people coming
        are nervous and scared and HOPE to feel better.
   (XV) The guide just puts the seed in your head of what
        you need to do.
   (XVI) Incredible empathy but does not get sucked in or
        own the problem
   (XVII) Brings out the light for us
   (XVIII) A way of challenging you... never once tossed
        away a question as stupid
   (XIX) With his permission I can give myself permission
   (XX) Opening options... things to hear

* The term relationship-centered awareness used here rec-ognizes that the HOPE Guide is conscious of the numerous relationships that influence what emerges, or is kept silent, within each meeting's experience. The relationships include each person's relationship with him or herself, their internal and external environments, and their story heretofore and as it is unfolding, to name a few.

Appendix G
The HOPE Guide Training Curriculum Outline

1) Describe the role of attitudinal healing in medicine and human care.
   a) The principles of attitudinal healing
      i) Love as the essence of being
         (1) Love is eternal and universal: we can choose to invite love to love through us
         (2) Love is a power or force that brings unity and wholeness to life
         (3) It is possible to learn to love ourselves and others
      ii) Health and healing arise from letting go
         (1) Release of fear and judgment
         (2) Embracing mutual care and respect
         (3) Wholeness emerges when we see ourselves and others in a peaceful and loving way
         (4) We are students and teachers to each other; we value the unique contributions each brings to life
         (5) A state of inner peace can be chosen and cultivated: that on which we focus manifests
      iii) Summarize the nature of compassion.
         (1) The transpersonal, spiritual nature of compassion
         (2) Contrast compassion, sympathy, empathy
         (3) Illustrate compassion in questions

       1. The power of questions in contrast to
           instructions
       2. The types of questions (open-closed) that can be
           asked
       3. The kinds of questions that express compassion
  (4) Identify cognitive, emotional, and physiological
      experiences with compassion
       1. A practical exercise of compassion directly
           applicable to medicine and health care
       2. The physiological effects of compassion
       3. The cognitive and emotional relationships with
           compassion

2) Reflect on the Guide's role, qualities, and participation in the
HOPE Group experience
a)   The Guide is one who knows that the possibility exists for
hopeful thoughts and attitudes
b)   The Guide is an exemplar of compassionate participation
that nurtures an environment of mutual care, consideration,
and safety
c)   The Guide is mature and because of self-awareness shares
his/her own emotional states and process
d)   The Guide is a catalyst for change and recognizes the
individual rhythms and strengths of those within the group
e)   The Guide illustrates HOPE Group process and the purpose
and functions of *The Gold Book*

3) Explain the ethical promise of hope in medical practice and
health care settings.
a)   Prognosis and compassion—possible or impossible?
b)   How might a physician/practitioner become
compassionately involved with the patient?
c)   What might be the effects of compassionate involvement
with patients?
d)   Students will examine these experiences and integrate them
into their personal life and professional practice.

i) Build a practice of reflection that facilitates this integration.

ii) Identify experiences of sharing and/or receiving compassion and a feeling of hope.

    (1) Explore the implications of promising the patient that (the physician) will do everything medically possible to help that person satisfy their "search for meaning" in their life.

    (2) Describes the effects of compassionate awareness and hope on self and the caring environment.

Authors' Biographical Notes

Ken Hamilton was born into a family of healers—medical, spiritual, and social—and has devoted his life to exploring the phenomenon of "healing." He chose the profession of medicine and received his medical degree from McGill University in 1960, moving on to complete a surgical residency in 1966. Both experiences comprised hard work in supportive, compassionate environments. Prior to responding to HOPE's call, he was active in statewide surgical and emergency medical organizations. After the call to HOPE, he became active in holistic and complementary medical circles with training in reiki, past-life regression, and shamanism. In 1989, he received the Jefferson Award for Community Service for his HOPE work. HOPE has been his life focus since then and over the last decade, he has actively focused on developing means to restore care to health care, firmly believing this to be the essence of "health care reform."

Joyce Murphy has had a lifelong relationship with the natural world. She honors the creative force of the universe and its many forms of expression. Joyce's passion for nature and the creative process has guided her along a path of holistic study and practice. She is a certified advanced Holistic Nurse and certified Healing Touch Practitioner who has been learning, practicing, and teaching holism and the use of complementary modalities for over 15 years. She supports individuals, families, and groups with methods to promote self-care and well being. Joyce teaches holistic practices that include use of the breath, guided imagery, creativity, and energy awareness. She is a long term member of the American Holistic Nurses' Association and serves the membership on the Leadership Council. Joyce works as a holistic nurse consultant and teaches nurse students across the country through the Distance Nursing Education Program at Saint Joseph's College of Maine.

Printed in the United States
203719BV00001B/589-600/A